VEG IN ONE BED

VEG IN ONE BED

HOW TO GROW AN ABUNDANCE OF FOOD
IN ONE RAISED BED, MONTH BY MONTH

HUW RICHARDS

CONTENTS

FOREWORD

I fell in love with growing food because it's a joy to eat home-grown produce. The flavour and quality of your own hand-picked vegetables is totally superior to anything you can buy from a shop, because there is no way to get food that is any fresher. Every summer I am again surprised by just how sweet home-grown peas taste straight from the pod.

There is also something magical about sowing a tiny seed and watching it grow to produce a delicious crop. You don't need green fingers and years of gardening experience to make this happen, but a little good advice will help to get you started; so I wrote this book to walk you through the simple steps needed to grow an abundance of food in a small area. If you have grown vegetables before, I hope the book will provide lots of practical hints and tips, as well as ideas to maximize the productivity of your space. If you are new to growing veg, don't worry, you will find all the information that you need to get started right here.

In this book, I have chosen to focus on cultivating a single raised bed, because for new gardeners a defined area is easier to manage. The 3 x 1.2m (10 x 4ft) dimensions of the bed make it large enough to grow a satisfying range and quantity of crops, but also compact enough to fit in even a small garden. I've also included tips for raising crops and seedlings on your windowsill, so you always have seedlings ready to replace finished crops in the bed.

The main plan shows you how to produce harvests from 19 different vegetables (yes, 19!) from your one raised bed in a single growing season. Month-by-month chapters clearly set out the essential tasks throughout the year, helping you to make sure that everything is on track. You will be amazed how little work is needed to produce so many different crops.

I wish you every success with your raised bed, and hope that by the end of the year you can't wait to start sowing again the following spring! I've added some ideas of new vegetables you can grow in the second year and beyond at the back of the book.

GETTING
STARTED

This is the beginning of your fantastic new vegetable-growing adventure. Before you start, there are a few things you will need to know, and I'll cover those topics in this chapter. I'll begin by showing you how to build your raised bed and what tools you'll need. Then I'll explain how you can plan for the weather, how to work out when your plants need watering, and of course, how to produce compost that will keep your bed bursting with nutrients.

THE **RAISED BED**

Raised beds can be found in all sorts of locations, sizes, and styles, and are a fantastic tool for vegetable growers. Let me convince you why I think raised beds help to make growing vegetables easy.

WHY USE A RAISED BED?

There are many reasons to grow vegetables in a raised bed:

• Size – this small, defined space is easily manageable when it comes to adding nutrients to the soil, staying on top of weeds and pests, and planning plant spacings.
• Practicality – being above the ground, a raised bed is easy to work in without standing on the soil and compacting it (*see right*).
• Microclimate – the soil in the bed will warm up more quickly than the ground in spring, and drain better after heavy rain.
• Convenience – raised beds are easy to build and take apart, which is especially useful if you are living in rented accommodation. They can even be built on paving slabs or concrete, allowing you to grow vegetables where there is no soil depth.

THE IDEAL SIZE FOR A RAISED BED

There are many opinions on the ideal size of a raised bed, but I have chosen 1.2 x 3m (4 x 10ft), as I feel it is perfect for starting your vegetable gardening journey – easy to build and fill with soil, and with plenty of space for growing. A depth of 30cm (1ft) will suit almost all vegetables.

WHEREVER YOU ARE
Raised beds can be built in almost any location, whether in a garden like mine (*see above*), on a hillside (*top left*), in an allotment (*top right*), in a backyard (*bottom right*), or even on a roof terrace or patio (*bottom left*).

FOR ME, THE BEST WAY TO START GROWING VEGETABLES IS IN A RAISED BED – THEY ARE PRACTICAL, MANAGEABLE, AND WILL HELP YOUR VEGETABLES TO THRIVE.

THE **WINDOWSILL**

Windowsills are a fantastic tool for gardeners, allowing them to maximize the productivity of their beds. Seeds can germinate and grow into seedlings on the windowsill, ready to be transplanted into the bed when there is space.

WHY USE A WINDOWSILL?

Sowing seeds in warm indoor conditions gives plants a useful head start on those sown directly into the raised bed. Not only can you get your harvest sooner and squeeze in extra autumn crops before winter (as plants require less growing time in the bed), but you can start tender, frost-sensitive crops earlier in the year, extending their growing season.

Sowing seeds indoors also protects young, vulnerable seedlings from pests, such as slugs and snails. By the time they are transplanted out, they will be much more resilient to pest damage.

When sowing seeds directly into a raised bed, you may find uneven gaps between plants due to sporadic germination, or that seedlings will need to be thinned out because they are too close together. The beauty of transplanting seedlings from the windowsill is that you can give plants the amount of space they need to grow. I also like the instant visual impact of transplanting strong, healthy seedlings into the bed.

Some plants are better suited to being sown directly into the bed, however, as they grow a long taproot that can easily be damaged if they are transplanted.

PLANTS ON THE WINDOWSILL
A windowsill full of pots and seedlings is an exciting sight, but remember to label your everything so that you don't forget what is what.

WHAT YOUR SEEDLINGS NEED

FIND A SUNNY SPOT

Choose the sunniest windowsill in your house on which to grow seedlings. Without direct sun, plants develop long, weak stems as they search for more light, and then won't stand up to outdoor conditions when transplanted into your bed. South-facing windowsills are best, followed by east-facing ones. If these are not available, add your own sunlight using LED grow lights, turned on for at least eight hours a day.

STABILIZE TEMPERATURES

The temperature on a windowsill is warmer and more consistent than outdoors, allowing seeds to germinate earlier in the season and seedlings to grow faster.

Also there aren't any frosts, which could damage or kill the more tender plants in your bed.

However, seedlings grown indoors are a little tender, and some need toughening up before they are ready to move outside. This can be done using a process called "hardening off" (*see panel below*).

PROVIDE AIR FLOW

When growing seedlings indoors, there is far less airflow and far more humidity around the plants. This creates the ideal conditions for fungal diseases, such as damping off, which can kill young seedlings. To counteract fungi, open the window briefly every day or two to give plants a nice flow of fresh air.

HARDENING OFF

This process toughens up young plants raised indoors by slowly introducing them to outdoor conditions, such as wind and cold weather. Hardened-off plants are less likely to suffer from shock and a period of slow growth after being transplanted. It is essential to harden off tender plants, such as runner beans, but all young plants will benefit from this introduction to life outside, especially if you live in a cold or windy area. I will admit to not hardening off all of my plants, but those I don't harden off take noticeably longer to get used to their new growing conditions.

The general method of hardening off plants is as follows:

1. For the first few days, place the seedlings outside during the day in a sheltered but sunny spot. Provide some shade for the first two days if the weather is hot. Bring them back inside at night.

2. After five to seven days, leave them outside overnight. Place fleece over the seedlings to keep them warm, but if there is any risk of frost bring them indoors. Don't forget to take off the fleece in the morning.

3. After ten days they will be ready for transplanting. Should there be a frost after they have been transplanted, protect them with a layer or two of horticultural fleece.

READY FOR THE OUTDOORS
Harden off tender plants to lessen the shock of outdoor conditions when they are transplanted. Don't worry if you miss a day or two; any hardening off will be beneficial.

WHAT **YOU NEED**

The great thing about growing plants in a raised bed is that you don't need lots of expensive equipment. I do recommend buying good-quality tools – look after them well and it will be a long time before you have to replace them.

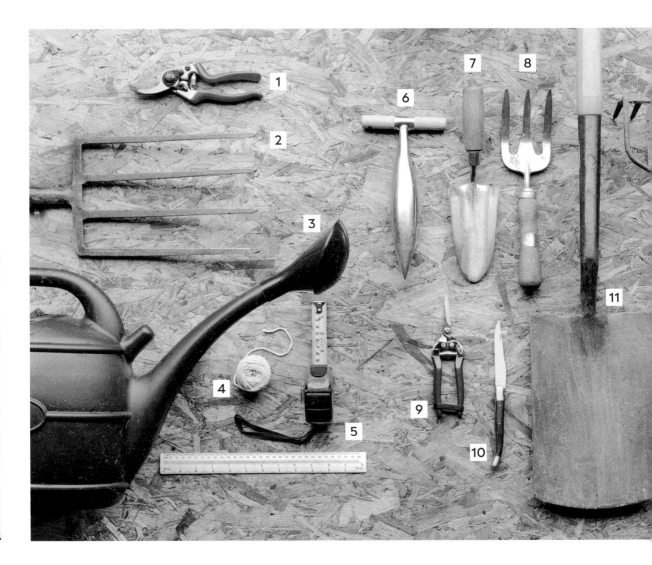

HOW TO SOURCE TOOLS

The best piece of advice I can give you is to buy quality tools. It's more expensive in the short term, but the difference in performance, feel, and durability more than makes up for this extra outlay.

You could borrow tools from or share them with a neighbour or friend. This cuts costs, and helps build friendships – as long as you both look after the tools!

LOOKING AFTER YOUR TOOLS

Make sure that your tools are stored inside when not in use. Cutting tools will quickly rust in the rain, and other tools will not last as long if left outdoors (or may simply get lost). If you use a cutting tool on diseased plants, sterilize it afterwards to avoid spreading disease. To do this, simply burn off any organic matter with an open flame, or wipe the tool well with disinfectant.

THE ESSENTIALS

If your budget is tight, you can get by with just a rake, spade, hand fork, knife, string, and your hands. However, I've listed everything I use below in case you want to invest.

1. Secateurs are robust scissors used for cutting spent stems, removing diseased growth, and pruning shrubby plants.

2. A fork is used to harvest leeks and potatoes, turn compost, and lift roots.

3. A watering can is a must-have. Fit the spout with a rose to diffuse the flow of water and reduce the risk of damaging or washing away your smaller plants when you water them.

4. String is used to mark out straight rows or tie climbing plants to their supports.

5. A ruler or tape measure is used to ensure that plant spacings are correct and to mark out straight lines.

6. A dibber is handy for creating holes in which to plant potatoes and leeks.

7. A trowel is used to dig small holes for transplanting, as well as for weeding and filling pots with compost.

8. A hand fork is useful for getting into small spaces to harvest vegetables or remove weeds.

9. Scissors are fantastic for harvesting vegetables such as dwarf beans and salad leaves, especially if you don't want to pull leaves or pods off the plant.

10. A knife is useful for cutting string and harvesting vegetables, especially if you don't have scissors to hand.

11. A spade helps when filling your raised bed with soil and compost.

12. A rake can be used to level and remove lumps from soil before sowing, and pick up leaves. The handle is useful for creating shallow trenches for sowing seeds.

THE OPTIONAL EXTRAS

• A sieve will allow you to create fine compost for sowing small seeds.
• Gloves are always welcome on a cold, wet day, although I rarely use them.

• Horticultural fleece (17g weight) protects plants down to -2°C (28°F), while allowing enough light through for them to grow. Double it up to protect down to -5°C (23°F).

• A wheelbarrow is perfect for moving soil and heavy bags of compost. It's also useful for collecting and moving leaves to add to your leaf mould pile.

YOUR **RAISED BED**

A rectangular raised bed, measuring 3 x 1.2m (10 x 4ft), is really straightforward to build and needn't be expensive either. It can be built in a garden or paved yard, or even on a roof terrace.

CHOOSE YOUR RAISED BED

WHAT YOU NEED

6 decking boards
(3m x 15cm/10ft x 6in)

tape measure

handsaw

8 posts
(60 x 5 x 5cm/
24 x 2 x 2in)

spirit level

spade

set square

electric drill with 4mm
(⅛in) drill bit and
screwdriver drill bit

40 countersunk
stainless steel screws
(80 x 5mm/3 x ¼in)

a spike, such as the
end of a chisel and
point crowbar

mallet

A quick online search brings up an overwhelming number of raised-bed styles to choose from. I always build my own beds, so I've given a list of possible building materials below. If you want your bed to sit on a hard surface, use a strong material, such as thick hardwood or bricks, as you won't be able to drive posts into the ground to reinforce the sides.

• Decking made from recycled plastic is my chosen material. It has a lifespan of around 100 years and doesn't leach chemicals into the soil.
• Scaffolding boards are a cheap option, but are narrow, and their their lifespan is only around five years. They are also too thin to easily double up for extra depth.
• Wooden boards made of sustainably sourced hardwood should be about 5cm (2in) thick. Treated wood lasts longer, but avoid chemicals that leach into the soil.
• Brick and mortar beds are long-lasting and strong, but need to be built on firm ground to prevent the walls from shifting.
• Galvanised steel sheets last well and can be screwed to corner posts. Sheets taller than 30cm (1ft) can be cut to size, or sunk into the ground for extra support.

BUILD YOUR OWN RAISED BED
To build your raised bed, have all your tools to hand before you start. If you can, find a willing helper, as this job is much easier with two people! The boards I used were only 15cm (6in) wide, so I doubled them up to get the 30cm (1ft) bed depth I wanted.

If your site is covered by particularly long grass or weeds, mow it before you start.

1. Keep four full boards for the long sides of the bed. For the ends, measure and cut four 1.2m (4ft) sections from the other two boards. Cut eight 60cm (2ft) posts to anchor the bed.

2. Lay the boards out flat on the ground and then balance the first layer of boards on their narrow edges. Use a spirit level, or smartphone app, to check that the boards are level.

3. Where the ground is uneven, dig a narrow trench using a spade so that the footprint of the raised bed is as level as possible.

4. Hold a long board with a short board butted up to the side of it at a 90-degree angle. A set square will help to ensure that you get a right angle.

CONTINUED >>

5. Drill pilot holes through one side of the long board, so that the screws can travel easily into the end of the short board. Then screw the long and short boards together. Repeat this process in the other corners to complete one layer of the bed. Repeat steps two to five to make another layer. Keep the two layers separate for now.

6. Position the first layer of the bed on your level ground and balance the second layer on top. Carefully place a spike just inside one of the corners and use a mallet to hammer it into the ground to make a hole about 30cm (1ft) deep. Replace the spike with a corner post and use the mallet to hammer it into the hole so that

the top of the post sits just below the top of the bed. Repeat for each corner. (If you are building your bed on a hard surface, cut down the posts to 30cm/1ft and place in the corners of the bed.)

7. Drill a pilot hole through the sides of the bed and screw the decking boards to the corner posts from outside in.

8. Use your spike and mallet to create a hole 1m (3ft) along one long side of the bed, and hammer a post into it. Then screw the post in place. Repeat 2m (6½ft) along the same side of the bed, and then 1m (3ft) and 2m (6½ft) along the other long side.

FILL YOUR RAISED BED

Different grades of topsoil are available, but try to buy topsoil enriched with organic matter, as this has the nutrients that your growing plants will need. If you can only get regular topsoil (without additions), fill the bed to about 8cm (3in) from the top, add a 5cm (2in) layer of peat-free multi-purpose compost, and mix the top 15–20cm (6–8in) of compost and soil together using a fork.

Check that the topsoil you buy has a slightly acidic pH. You can do this by testing it with a simple kit available from garden centres. A pH of 6.5 suits most vegetables perfectly, but any reading that is between 6 and 7.5 will be fine. It's rare for topsoil to be outside this range, but it's definitely worth checking before you buy.

A cubic-metre (220-gallon) bag of topsoil (get one delivered) is perfect for a 3 x 1.2 x 0.3m (10 x 4 x 1ft) bed, as it will leave a gap of about 5cm (2in) between the soil and the top of the bed.

SOIL AND COMPOST
I fill my beds using regular topsoil and peat-free, multi-purpose compost, mixing it together to ensure that the nutrients are spread out evenly.

SEEDS AND SEEDLINGS

When starting off plants, you can choose to buy seeds or seedlings. You will also need to decide which variety you want to grow, where you are going to buy it, and what you are going to sow or plant it in.

SEEDS OR SEEDLINGS?

The most affordable way of raising vegetables is to grow them yourself from seed – I start everything I can this way. This requires a little more effort, compost, and a few more pots, but seed is cheap, can be sown multiple times each season, and will usually remain viable for a few years (look at the expiry date on each packet to check when germination rates will decrease). You can also find the full range of vegetable varieties as seeds, whereas seedling choices are more limited.

Seedlings, on the other hand, are reliable and save time, which can be helpful if a sowing fails. Seedlings are also a good option if you only want a few plants for a particular crop – buying some seedlings won't cost you much more than buying a packet of seeds.

Some vegetables shouldn't be started off from seedlings, such as root vegetables, because they can be badly affected by being transplanted. These plants should be grown *in situ* from seed.

WHICH VARIETY?

Almost all vegetables are available in different named varieties, each of which has been selected for its own useful qualities, such as high yield, early maturity, or good flavour. Choosing between varieties can be difficult, but be sure to consider the size of the plant and its suitability for your local climate. F1 hybrids are varieties specially bred for their vigour and uniformity, and tend to be more expensive. If you're not sure which to go for, I'll list my favourite, readily available varieties whenever I mention a new vegetable in this book. It's also worth remembering that the best-selling varieties are popular for a reason.

VARIATIONS ON A THEME
Different varieties of a vegetable can look and taste different. Take these examples of curly kale (*left*) and red kale (*right*).

WHERE TO BUY?

Vegetable seeds are widely available to buy – supermarkets, home-improvement retailers, and hardware stores will stock a few varieties of the most common vegetables. If you're looking for seedlings or a specific variety of a plant, try a garden centre or online specialist supplier (remember to order in advance of when you need to plant if buying online). See p223 for a list of my recommended suppliers.

In autumn, many large retailers drop the price of their vegetable seeds to make way for new stock. Join a local gardening group or an online gardening page to be the first to hear when a clearance is happening.

SPOTTING UNHEALTHY SEEDLINGS

Choosing strong, healthy seedlings is a key skill when buying plants or selecting those to transplant into your bed. Healthy seedlings are bright green, with strong, upright stems, no marks on the leaves, and a good network of fine, white roots if you push them gently from their module.

THE BAD AND THE GOOD
With large leaves and visible roots, the seedling on the right looks much healthier than that on the left, despite both being sown at the same time.

POTS AND SEED TRAYS

Many kinds of containers can be used to raise seeds and seedlings. Where possible, I use recycled materials:

- Use newspaper pots (*see p142*) or cardboard loo roll tubes to start plants that dislike root disturbance. Seedlings can be transplanted in the pot or tube, which will decompose in the soil.

- Ice cream tubs are useful for holding newspaper pots and loo roll tubes. Add drainage holes to use them as seedtrays (*see below*).

- Egg boxes for chitting potatoes (*see p49*).

Shop-bought items

I have also bought a few good-quality items that have lasted for many years. Look out for pots and trays made from biodegradable materials, such as bamboo.

1. Module trays are divided into small sections (modules) and are used to raise plants individually from seed.

2. Pots are available in a range of sizes. Use them to grow on seedlings that have outgrown modules.

3. Seed trays are open trays that are ideal for starting seeds or growing microgreens on a windowsill.

PLAN FOR **THE WEATHER**

Harnessing as much sunlight as possible will provide fantastic rewards when it comes to growing vegetables. You'll need to protect your crops from harsher weather, however, so check local forecasts for strong winds and frosts.

WATCH OUT FOR FROST

Temperatures fluctuate considerably outdoors, from day to night, season to season, and with the weather. The biggest threat comes from frosts, which can damage plants unable to tolerate low temperatures.

Plants are given a rating based on their "hardiness", or ability to withstand cold. Knowing how hardy your crops are and planning accordingly will prevent you losing any carefully raised seedlings to frosts, especially those that occur during autumn and winter. The different levels of plant hardiness are as follows:

• Hardy vegetables are generally able to withstand frosts down to -8°C (18°F) with no protection. However, these temperatures may damage leaves and cause plants to die back. Examples are broad beans and kale.
• Half-hardy vegetables can tolerate frost for a few hours, but will not survive long periods of cold outside over winter. They include peas, beetroot, and lettuce.
• Tender vegetables are heat-loving crops that are damaged by even the lightest frost. Runner beans, dwarf French beans, and tomatoes are all tender.

Keep all your tender vegetables indoors until the risk of frost has passed (look up the average date of the first and last frost in your area online). I always check the minimum forecasted temperature every night during early spring, and if it is 4°C (39°F) or below, I protect plants with a layer of horticultural fleece, bubble wrap, or an old bed sheet. If you follow the growing plan in this book, you will only need to protect your potatoes, but frost protection will be a must for other plans.

UNDER THE COVERS
Cover plants with 17g horticultural fleece to protect them at temperatures of 4°C (39°F) down to -2°C (28°F). Using two layers will protect them down to -5°C (23°F).

PROTECT FROM WIND

Strong winds can damage plants, especially when they have just been transplanted, so find a sheltered spot for your raised bed where possible. In gardens with existing walls and hedges, there should be enough windbreaks to prevent any problems. Consider planting a hedge to diffuse damaging gusts in more exposed gardens.

SHELTER AND SUPPORT
Give your raised bed as much shelter as you can, and support plants with canes if necessary.

MAXIMIZE SUNLIGHT

The position of the raised bed will have a direct impact on its productivity. Most vegetables do best in full sun, so build your bed in the sunniest part of your garden and angle it so that its long edges face south. This prevents the vegetables from shading each other as the sun moves during the day. Angling the long edges of the bed to face south-east is the next best option, followed by facing them east.

If you have a "sun trap" created by a south-facing wall or fence, then place the north edge of your bed close to this boundary to provide a warmer microclimate for your vegetables. This is because walls and fences absorb sunlight throughout the day, and then radiate heat during the evening and night. They will also help to shield the bed from winds that carry away warm air. Don't worry if you don't have the ideal location for your bed, because six hours of direct sunlight each day will be enough for most vegetables.

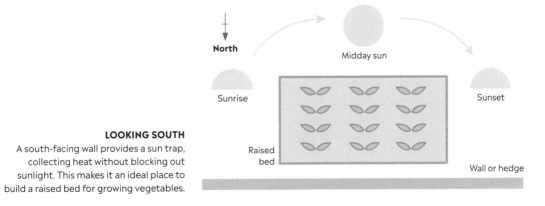

North

Midday sun

Sunrise

Sunset

Raised bed

Wall or hedge

LOOKING SOUTH
A south-facing wall provides a sun trap, collecting heat without blocking out sunlight. This makes it an ideal place to build a raised bed for growing vegetables.

WATER YOUR CROPS

All plants need water to grow and, as in humans, too much or too little water can cause health problems. Plants, however, are much more resilient than us when it comes to water scarcity.

WATER YOUR BED

Healthy, mature plants that have been well watered should be able to survive a few weeks without being watered again (although ideally I'd water more often than that). It takes a lot of hot weather to take moisture out of deep soil, but the soil near the surface dries out relatively quickly. Even if the surface of the soil looks dry, dig down a bit and you will soon reach moisture. If you need to dig down 5cm (2in) or more to find moisture, then it is time to water your raised bed.

Each time you water, empty four full watering cans into your raised bed, giving more water to shallow-rooted plants, such as lettuce. Lettuce roots grow close to the surface, so it's important to ensure that they don't dry out. This is especially true during the summer, as warm, dry weather can cause vegetables to flower or run to seed (known as "bolting"), ruining the flavour. It's also important to prioritize watering your beans and peas, as these are most vulnerable to drought-related problems, such as not producing pods.

For young seedlings, water from just above the leaves to reduce any potential damage to the plant, or change the rose of your watering can so that it produces a finer spray of water. If hail is forecast, cover the seedlings with fleece to prevent damage.

Raised beds drain freely so don't get waterlogged. I've never lost a plant in my beds due to excess water – even with all the rain we get where I live in Wales!

A GOOD SOAK
Water when the soil is dry to 5cm (2in) below the surface. Four full watering cans should be more than enough water for one bed.

WATER YOUR SEEDLINGS

One question I'm often asked is "When should I water my seedlings?" Seedlings on the windowsill have only a small root system, and will struggle if required to go more than a day in dried-out compost. On the other hand, overwatering seedlings can also cause them to die. It is better to water too little than too often.

To work out if you need to water your seedlings, poke your finger into the compost to about 2cm (¾in) deep. If there is no moisture at this point, then it is a good idea to water the plant. I find that in hot weather I need to water my seedlings every day, and in cool weather every two to three days.

The quantity of water you give your seedlings also matters. The surface may look wet, but there may not be any moisture around the roots. To ensure there is enough water for your plants, water until around three seconds after you first see liquid leaking from the base of the pot or container.

A LIGHT SHOWER
It's easier to water seedlings with a smaller watering vessel with a fine spray. I used a converted plastic bottle (*see panel below*).

MAKE A WATERING BOTTLE

A standard watering can is far too large to easily water seedlings. A convenient alternative is to use a converted plastic bottle. A 500ml (16fl oz) bottle is easy to move around one-handed as it isn't too heavy, is also easy to fill with water, and can produce a fine spray of water.

1. Take the cap off the bottle, and ensure that the bottle has no liquid inside.

2. Create five or six holes in the cap using a hammer and nail, or some sort of strong, sharp point. Take care when making holes, tapping gently with the hammer and making sure that you don't cause injury or damage.

3. Fill the bottle with water, put the cap back on, and turn it upside down to water your seedlings. This will provide a gentle flow of water. You can make the holes in the bottle cap wider to increase the flow of water if required.

A SECOND LIFE
Used plastic bottles can have a second longer life as watering cans for seedlings.

THE **COMPOST BIN**

You can't have a vegetable garden without some kind of composting system. Compost is so important in the garden that it is widely known to gardeners as "black gold". The good news is that you can make your own!

WHY USE COMPOST?

Compost is simply decayed organic matter that is full of nutrients, and is used as a fertilizer to enrich the soil where plants are grown. To give you an idea of the importance of compost, here is a list of garden tasks that I use it for:

• When I sow seeds in modules or seed trays, I plant them into 100 per cent compost or a 50/50 mix of compost and soil. This is because seedlings love the high nutrient content that compost provides.
• When transplanting seedlings into my raised beds, I will sometimes dig a hole and then add a large handful or two of compost before putting the seedling in place. This provides a boost of nutrients that says "Welcome to your new home!"
• In preparation for spring, I will add a 5–10cm (2–4in) layer of compost to my pots and raised beds in late autumn, and then cover empty parts of my raised beds over winter (*see pp182–183*). This leaves weed-free, nutrient-rich soil when uncovered at the beginning of the growing season.

Once your raised bed is set up, you won't need much compost to keep it going, so you should be able to produce all the compost you need yourself.

LEAFING THROUGH
Leaves are brown compost materials (*see opposite*). There are always plenty around in autumn, which you can add to your compost bin, or to a separate leaf-mould bin (*see p163*).

THE SMALLER THE PIECE OF MATERIAL, THE FASTER IT WILL DECOMPOSE, SO TEAR UP LARGE PIECES OF CARDBOARD!

HOW TO COMPOST

There are two types of compost materials: green and brown. Green compost materials are rich in nitrogen. Some examples are:
• Animal manure (not dog or cat manure)
• Grass clippings
• Coffee grounds
• Brewery grains
• Vegetable scraps or spent plants
• Young weeds (avoid weeds that have flowered or gone to seed, as you will effectively be spreading their seeds around your garden)

Brown compost materials are rich in carbon. Some examples are:
• Autumn leaves
• Small branches from garden prunings
• Shredded paper or newspaper
• Cardboard

For every bucketful of greens you add to your compost pile, you want to add two buckets of browns. Apply greens and browns in layers like lasagne (green, brown, green, etc.) This "lasagne" method is great for "slow composting", which can take anywhere from 6 to 18 months, depending on the materials you use.

For a speedier turnaround, turn your compost pile every month or two using a fork. This introduces oxygen into the pile, which speeds up the rate at which microorganisms break down materials.

Bear in mind that there are a few things you shouldn't add to your compost pile:
• Fish and meat scraps, which attract rats
• Citrus fruits, which make the soil too acidic, killing off worms and microorganisms that break down compost materials
• Tea bags, which contain plastic
• Chemically treated wood and glossy or coated paper, which leach harmful chemicals into the soil

It's also worth keeping large woody branches and cuttings separate, as these will take a lot longer to decompose than smaller, softer materials.

SOURCING COMPOSTING MATERIALS LOCALLY

As well as your own home, there are a variety of places from which to source composting materials. Try approaching neighbours or family and friends for vegetable scraps, grass clippings, leaves, and cardboard – suburban areas are ideal for this.

In autumn there are always plenty of leaves around. You could try phoning your local council to ask whether they will let you collect a few bags of leaves from a nearby park.

I find that I often have particular luck going to local businesses, such as shops, pubs, and cafes. They often have cardboard boxes, coffee grounds, or vegetable scraps that they are willing to give me. Approach whoever is in charge, and don't be afraid to barter for something. In our society, many of us have forgotten the concept of exchanging resources without money.

COMMON COMPOSTING PROBLEMS

These are some common composting problems and how to fix them:

• Smelly compost is usually a problem if there is too much nitrogen and/or not enough oxygen in your pile. Add lots of brown materials and mix them in to resolve the problem. Keep a layer of browns on top to mask the smell.

• Wet compost is a problem in areas that get a lot of rain. Keep your compost in a covered bin – a slab of wood will work well if you are using a home-made compost bin.

• Slow composting is often caused by a lack of moisture or an excess of brown waste. If you think your compost is too dry, adding a couple of watering cans of water should do the trick. If there is too much brown material, mix in a few bucketfuls of greens, or dig a hole in the centre of the pile and drop the greens into the middle.

CHOOSE YOUR COMPOST BIN

WHAT YOU NEED

4 pallets of
the same size

heavy-duty wire
or string

hammer and nails or
screwdriver and
screws (optional)

4 wooden posts to fit
between pallet slats
(optional)

mallet (optional)

chicken wire

staple nails

wire cutters

While you could just keep your compost in a pile at the back of the garden, you are more likely to want a bin to put it in and keep things tidy. I like wooden compost bins, as they can add real character to a garden. Almost any kitchen garden or allotment you go to will have a wooden compost bin tucked away in a corner – we have five in our garden!

There are many different types of compost bin available. Here are some options for you to choose from:

• Wooden, flat-pack compost bins are an easy option if you have tough ground or don't fancy digging holes. They are easy to put together, and don't need any nails or screws. I like the beehive-style versions, which I think look good in any garden.

• Plastic compost bins are ideal for small spaces. The lid will keep in heat and moisture to aid decomposition, and they can be placed on a hard surface. They often have an opening at the base so that you can take decomposed material from the bottom of the pile.

• Tumblers are compost bins that you can spin. This is an easy way of turning the compost to ensure everything is well mixed. However, they have limited capacity and turning can be hard work when they are full.

• Home-made compost bins are great, and can often be made cheaply from scraps of wood or metal (I use pallets to make mine). They can be made to a size that suits your needs, and to fit in the space you have available. Cover your home-made bin with an old sheet of plywood or tarpaulin to protect your compost from the rain.

BUILD YOUR OWN COMPOST BIN

This simple box is lined with chicken wire to prevent decomposing materials from falling out of the pile, and has a door at the front to allow easy access to your compost. When you have built your compost bin, move it to a quiet spot on soil or lawn. If you run out of space, you can easily add more bays with a few extra pallets.

1. Stand three pallets on end to form three sides of a cube. The fourth pallet should fill the gap at the front perfectly, and will act as the door.

2. Lash the corners of the first three pallets together tightly with heavy-duty wire or string, tying them at the top and bottom where they meet. You could also screw or nail them together if you prefer. If you are building your compost bin on sloping ground, add stability by driving posts down through the central gap in the pallets using a mallet.

3. Line the inside of the three joined pallets with chicken wire, and attach it by hammering in the staple nails. Then cut off any excess wire. Do the same for the fourth pallet.

4. Slot the fourth pallet into the gap to form a door. Loosely tie it to one side with the string to form a hinge, then tie the other side with a quick-release knot. This will keep the door in place, but still allow easy access.

YOUR BED
MONTH
BY MONTH

This is where the fun starts, as I lead you through a detailed plan for your first year of growing vegetables. Covering the entire year month by month, I will show you everything you need to do on your windowsill and in your raised bed to start, grow, and harvest 19 different crops. Each month starts with an "At a glance" overview to use as a quick reference, before you dive into the more detailed instructions that follow.

YEAR PLANNER

This chart shows what is happening in each part of the bed during the year. The bed is divided up into ten sections along its length, each 30cm (1ft) wide and labelled one to ten. These sections are referred to throughout the book (especially look out for them in the "On the plan" diagrams at the beginning of each month), so you may want mark them in your own bed using string and/or plant labels or old yoghurt pots.

ON YOUR WINDOWSILL

Month	Start off
March	Pea shoots Broad beans
April	Leeks Runner beans
May	Dwarf French beans Kale
June	Peas
July	Lettuce
August	Kohl rabi Swiss chard
September	Chinese cabbage
November	Microgreens

IN YOUR RAISED BED

SECTION	MARCH	APRIL	MAY
1	**Potatoes** Sow	**Potatoes** Grow on	**Potatoes** Earth up
2			
3		**Broad beans** Transplant	**Broad beans** Tie in and grow on
4			
5	**Lettuce** Sow	**Lettuce** Thin and grow on	**Lettuce** Harvest
6			**Swiss chard** Sow
7			
8			**Runner beans** Transplant
9			
10	**Radish** Sow	**Radish** Harvest	

	JUNE	JULY	AUGUST	SEPTEMBER	OCTOBER	NOVEMBER	DEC–FEB
	Potatoes Harvest / **Leeks** Transplant	**Leeks** Grow on				**Leeks** Mulch	**Leeks** Harvest
	Broad beans Cut off tops	**Broad beans** Harvest / **Kale** Transplant	**Kale** Tie in and grow on		**Kale** Harvest	**Kale** Mulch	
		Radish Sow and harvest	**Lettuce** Transplant	**Lettuce** Harvest	**Chinese cabbage** Transplant	**Chinese cabbage** Harvest / Mulch and cover with cardboard	Mulch and cover with cardboard
	Swiss chard Grow on	**Swiss chard** Harvest ·	**Kohl rabi** Transplant	**Kohl rabi** Grow on		**Kohl rabi** Harvest	Mulch and cover with cardboard
	Beetroot Sow	**Beetroot** Thin and grow on		**Beetroot** Harvest / **Mustard** Sow	**Mustard** Harvest		Mulch and cover with cardboard
		Turnips Sow	**Turnips** Thin and grow on	**Turnips** Harvest		Mulch and cover with cardboard	
			Carrots Sow	**Carrots** Thin and grow on		**Carrots** Harvest	Mulch and cover with cardboard
	Runner beans Train and grow on		**Runner beans** Harvest	**Spinach** Sow	**Spinach** Harvest	**Spinach** Mulch	**Spinach** Grow on
	Dwarf French beans Transplant	**Dwarf French beans** Grow on	**Dwarf French beans** Harvest	**Swiss chard** Transplant	**Swiss chard** Harvest	**Swiss chard** Mulch	**Swiss chard** Grow on
	Radish Harvest	**Peas** Transplant	**Peas** Harvest		**Garlic** Sow	**Garlic** Grow on	

KEY — Empty · Start off · Transplant · Grow on · Harvest

MARCH

BEST THING ABOUT MARCH
Planting your chitted
potatoes in the raised bed

WORST THING ABOUT MARCH
Conditions can remain cold,
limiting what you can grow

WATCH OUT FOR IN MARCH
The first tender green shoots
of a new growing season

GETTING A FAST START
Even though there can be some pretty dismal, cold, and wet weather in March, the raised bed allows any excess rainwater to drain away quickly and lets the soil to warm up faster than the ground around it. This allows you to get out into your garden as early as possible.

Lettuces
Two rows of tiny lettuce seedlings should be beginning to appear by the end of March

Radishes
By the end of the month your small radish seedlings will form a lovely orderly row

MARCH AT A GLANCE

March is the first glimpse of a new growing season, but is often still cold, meaning some seeds are best sown indoors for transplanting later in spring. However, you will get a taste of working in your raised bed this month, as you will be sowing lettuce and radish, and planting potatoes.

HOW THE BED WILL LOOK
In its first month, the appearance of the bed won't change a great deal from the bare soil you began with. The first tiny seedlings will peep through a few weeks after sowing, towards the end of the month, but their growth will be a little slow this early in spring.

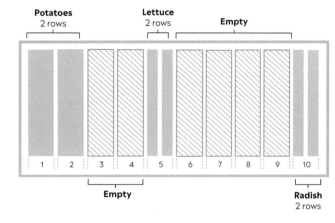

Potatoes
2 rows

Lettuce
2 rows

Empty

ON THE PLAN
The bed's transformation begins this month as crops are gradually sown and planted into the empty soil. This plan makes it easy to fit many crops into the raised bed during the year.

KEY

 Empty

Start off

1 : Section number

1 2 3 4 5 6 7 8 9 10

Empty

Radish
2 rows

ON THE WINDOWSILL
Start off
• Sow a tray thickly with peas for a quick crop of shoots. Keep the tray well watered and turn it daily to prevent the shoots bending towards the light.
• Sow broad beans in cardboard tubes to make planting out easy. Water regularly to keep the compost moist. Turn them so that they grow straight.

Harvest
• Pick pea shoots as and when you want them by pinching off the stems with your fingers or cutting them with scissors.

IN THE RAISED BED
Start off
• Sow a row of fast-growing radish seeds directly into section ten of your raised bed. Two weeks later, sow a second row. This will give you a longer, staggered harvest.
• Sow lettuce seeds thinly along two rows in section five to give you your first salad crop in May.
• Plant out two rows of chitted seed potatoes in sections one and two, being careful not to damage their shoots, once the soil has warmed up in the spring sunshine.

MAINTENANCE CHECKLIST
• Weed.
• Water.
• Watch out for slugs and snails when new shoots emerge.

PLACE A LARGE TRAY UNDERNEATH THE POTS OF SEEDLINGS YOU ARE GROWING ON YOUR WINDOWSILL, TO CATCH ANY SPILLS OF WATER OR COMPOST.

ON YOUR WINDOWSILL

Take advantage of the warmth on your windowsill to get spring vegetables off to an early start and grab a quick crop of pea shoots. Broad bean seeds sown now will be ready to transplant next month.

START OFF
PEA SHOOTS

SEED TO HARVEST
2–3 weeks

POSITION
Warm, sunny windowsill

WATER
Every 2–3 days

HARVEST
March
(All year round from successional sowings)

Peas aren't just grown for pods; their delicious young shoots are also a fantastic quick crop. You can grow pea shoots on a windowsill all year round – start them now and they will be the first crop you harvest.

The seeds are sown thickly, so you can expect a 20 x 30cm (8 x 12in) seed tray to produce an impressive 250g (9oz) of pea shoots, which makes this a really productive crop for a small space. Pea seeds can be quite expensive, so try using a large packet of dried peas from a grocery shop as a cheaper alternative. Their shoots will taste just as delicious.

1

SOWING PEAS FOR SHOOTS

You can grow pea shoots in any container with drainage holes, but a wide, shallow tray works best because they only need a compost depth of around 5cm (2in). Invest in a good-quality seed tray and it will last you for many years. Seeds are sown very thickly, so that they are almost touching, This is not a problem because you will be harvesting the young plants, so they don't need space to grow to maturity. Peas will germinate faster in warm conditions, so position them on a sunny windowsill in a heated room and don't shut them behind curtains at night. Shoot tips should emerge from the soil in around three to five days.

2

MAKE YOUR OWN PLANT LABELS

Rather than going out and buying new plastic plant labels, try making your own from old yoghurt pots and ice cream tubs. You can then write on the names of your vegetable varieties with a permanent marker. This reuses plastic packaging and saves you money.

CUT YOUR COSTS
Use scissors to cut an old yoghurt pot or ice cream tub into 7 x 2cm (3 x ¾in) strips.

3

1. An hour before sowing the dried peas, place them in a container and fill it with water. Allowing them to soak up the moisture helps them germinate more quickly.

2. Cover the base of your seed tray with a 5cm (2in) layer of multi-purpose compost. Drain the excess water from your soaked peas and sprinkle them thickly over the surface of the compost, so that there is about a pea's width between them as a guide. Each pea will give you a shoot.

3. Cover the peas with a 1cm (½in) layer of compost, water thoroughly, and allow the tray to drain. Place in a warm, sunny position, and make sure that the compost does not dry out.

START OFF
BROAD BEANS

SEED TO TRANSPLANT
4–6 weeks

POSITION
Cool, bright windowsill

WATER
Every 2–3 days

TRANSPLANT
Mid-April

HARVEST
July

HUW'S TOP VARIETIES
'Bunyard's Exhibition'
'Crimson Flowered'
'Hangdown Green'

Broad beans are an excellent crop for any garden. They are easy to grow, productive, and their roots add nitrogen to the soil, helping to keep it in good health. These hardy plants need little attention once planted out, except perhaps some support to help keep them standing in high winds; this should be put in place during May, once the plants have grown taller.

SOWING BROAD BEANS

One of my favourite ways to sow broad beans in mid-March is into the cardboard tubes from the centre of loo rolls. It works well because you can transplant the whole seedling and tube out into the raised bed, where the tube will slowly decompose without disturbing the delicate, long roots.

These large beans can also be sown into deep pots, or special plastic containers called "root trainers", designed to give their long roots space to grow.

DON'T WORRY ABOUT ACCIDENTALLY PLANTING A SEED UPSIDE DOWN. GRAVITY ENSURES THAT THE SEED WILL AUTOMATICALLY CORRECT THE DIRECTION IN WHICH ITS ROOT AND SHOOT GROW.

1

2

1. Collect about 18 cardboard tubes, to allow for some spare seedlings, or in case any seeds fail to grow. Fit the tubes into containers, such as old ice cream tubs or a tray, so that they stand upright. Fill the tubes up to about 1cm (½in) from the top with multi-purpose compost.

2. Push your finger into the compost to create a 2.5cm (1in) deep hole, and drop in a broad bean seed.

3. Fill the hole with compost using your fingers. Repeat to plant beans in all 18 tubes and water them thoroughly, until you see water begin to seep from the base of the tubes. Place the broad bean pots on your windowsill, water them every two to three days, and seedlings should emerge within two weeks.

3

MULTI-CROPPING PEAS
Harvesting just above the lowest leaf on the stem will ensure that the plant gives you a second crop.

HARVEST
PEA SHOOTS

Once the forest of green shoots has reached 6–7cm (2½–2¾in) tall, your pea shoots are ready to harvest. Pick them as you need them, by pinching off the shoots using your fingers, or cutting sections with scissors. If they are harvested above the lowest leaf on the stem, the shoots will regrow to give you a second crop. Once the crop is finished, tip what remains of the roots and compost on to your compost heap, and repeat the growing process again for another crop of shoots.

Pea shoots taste like fresh peas, with less sweetness, which is a delicious fresh flavour to have this early in spring.

HARVESTING YOUR FOREST OF PEA SHOOTS IS ALWAYS SATISFYING; YOU CAN USE SCISSORS TO CUT WHAT YOU NEED EXACTLY WHEN YOU NEED IT, AND HAVE THE FLAVOUR OF FRESH PEAS ON DEMAND IN EARLY SPRING.

IN YOUR RAISED BED

Seeing your first crops sown into the perfectly prepared soil of your bed makes March an exciting month. Your radish seedlings will emerge to produce the first row of green shoots later in the month.

START OFF
RADISH

SEED TO HARVEST
4 weeks

PLANTING DISTANCE
5mm (¼in) apart

LIGHT
Full sun to light shade

HARDINESS
Moderately hardy

KEY PROBLEMS
Flea beetle
Slugs and snails

HARVEST
April

HUW'S TOP VARIETIES
'Cherry Belle'
'Icicle'
'Purple Plum'

Radish is perhaps the easiest vegetable you can grow because, just four weeks after sowing, it is ready to harvest without any maintenance. This rapid growth means that radishes easily out-compete weeds. Any variety of fast-maturing summer radish will work, and when picked young and fresh, the roots are juicy with a hint of heat.

SOWING RADISHES

Sow the seeds into a shallow trench, also known as a drill, across the width of the bed in section ten of the bed (*see diagram, p37*). For a succession of radishes to harvest from mid-April to mid-May, sow your first row in mid-March and another row next to it two weeks later.

1

2

3

4

1. Tie a 1.2m (4ft) length of string to two sticks and use it to mark out a straight line across the width of section ten of the raised bed. Pull a rake handle or cane along the length of string, creating a wide trench around 1cm (½in) deep.

2. Sprinkle your radish seeds along the trench using your thumb and forefinger, as you would for a pinch of salt. Try to sow evenly, spacing seeds about ½cm (¼in) apart. The radish plants will push away from each other as they grow.

3. Cover the trench lightly with soil using your hand, and label your row to mark its position and remind you which variety you have sown.

4. Water with a watering can fitted with a rose. Soak each section of soil for two seconds before moving up the row.

PROTECT FROM BIRDS

Although birds help to control garden pests, they can also feast on your sown seeds and the leaves of growing vegetables. Preventing bird damage is simple, but does require investment in the right kit (*see pp218–219*).

Bird netting

This is the best way to protect crops, but good-quality netting is expensive. Buy netting that is 1.8–2.4m (6–8ft) wide so that it will cover tall plants. Protect all of your vulnerable crops by placing canes topped with plant pots at the corners of the bed nearest the potatoes, and 2.3m (7½ft) along the long edge of the bed, to leave space for the runner bean wigwam. Lay the netting over the top, and secure its edges with pegs or bricks.

If a bird becomes trapped in the netting, wear gloves while you let it out or cut the netting to free its legs.

KEEP BIRDS OUT
Prevent birds from eating your crops by keeping them out with netting.

START OFF

LETTUCE

SEED TO HARVEST
8 weeks

PLANTING DISTANCE
15cm (6in) apart

LIGHT
Full sun to partial shade

HARDINESS
Moderately hardy

KEY PROBLEMS
Slugs and snails

HARVEST
May

HUW'S TOP VARIETIES
'Buttercrunch'
'Freckles'
'Little Gem'
'Salad Bowl'
'Saladin'

Growing lettuce is fast and simple, and is a fantastic way to save money, because a single packet of seed has the potential to produce plentiful fresh leaves for a month or more. Salad leaves always taste so much sweeter when they have been freshly picked, just minutes before eating. There's a huge diversity of shape and colour in lettuce varieties, from "loose-leaf" types with open heads of leaves, to "hearting" varieties with their leaves layered closely in a dense head. You can choose exactly which ones you want to fill your salad bowl.

SOWING LETTUCE

Sowing lettuce along a drill is the best option if you want to grow a dense row of small plants to harvest continuously over several weeks. Lettuce seedlings can also be started on the windowsill (*see pp102–103*) to transplant into the bed, where they can instantly fill gaps left by harvesting other crops.

1

2

THE YOUNGER THE LETTUCE SEEDS ARE, THE FASTER THEY WILL GERMINATE. ALWAYS USE THE FRESHEST POSSIBLE SEEDS AND YOU WILL GET GOOD RESULTS.

3

1. Find the edge of section five by measuring 1.2m (4ft) from the opposite end of your raised bed to where you planted your radishes, and then mark a point 8cm (3in) on from there. Pull a 1.2m (4ft) string line across the width of the bed at the point you marked, and use a rake handle or cane to create a trench that is 1cm (½in) deep in the soil along it. Make a second trench 15cm (6in) on from the first.

2. Sprinkle the lettuce seeds thinly along the trenches. Try to sow on a still day, because strong winds can blow away the seeds. Label the rows and give them a good water from a watering can fitted with a rose.

3. Use your hand to gently cover the trenches with the soil that had been pushed aside by the rake handle or cane.

SLUGS AND SNAILS

Extremely annoying pests for vegetable gardeners, slugs and snails cause the destruction of seedlings and leafy crops, sometimes astonishingly quickly. Taking steps to control their numbers will make growing your own vegetables more enjoyable and productive (see pp218–219).

The slug pub

Slugs seem to love beer, so try setting a beer trap for them. Follow the steps below and check the next morning to see if you've caught any.

1. Bury a clean glass jar in the middle of the raised bed, or 30cm (1ft) away from your row of seedlings.

2. Push soil in around the outside of the jar so that it's stable, and fill it three-quarters full with cheap lager.

3. Make a small roof out of a piece of wood and some sticks in case it rains.

A TEMPTING TRAP
Slugs often fall into the jar after drinking the beer, and are unable to escape.

1

2

START OFF
POTATOES

**PLANTING
TO HARVEST**
10 weeks for "first
early" varieties

LIGHT
Full sun

PLANTING DISTANCE
30cm (1ft) apart

HARDINESS
Frost tender

KEY PROBLEMS
Slugs and snails
Blight

HARVEST
June

**HUW'S TOP
VARIETIES**
'Colleen'
'Maris Bard'
'Red Duke of York'
'Swift'

Potatoes are a must-have for any garden. They might be cheap to buy, but freshly harvested, home-grown new potatoes have a flavour that simply is not available in the shops. They are no trouble to grow either, although they cannot tolerate frost, so give them a head start by buying a pack of ten seed potatoes in February and getting their shoots growing indoors, known as "chitting" (*see panel opposite*). Choose the fastest-maturing varieties, known as "first earlies", which will be ready to harvest by the end of June. Don't plant them out until the soil is warming in the early spring sun, from mid to late March.

PLANTING SEED POTATOES
Traditionally, potatoes are planted in a trench lined with manure or compost. You can plant straight into the raised bed, however, because the soil has already been improved with compost, and will contain enough nutrients already. Be careful not to damage the shoots on your seed potatoes when handling them. Once they are planted, you should notice leaves emerging from beneath the soil in around four weeks. These will need protection from any late spring frosts. Your first new potatoes will be ready to harvest in June.

3

CHIT POTATOES

Potatoes are grown not by sowing seed, but by planting specially stored tubers (known as seed potatoes). Before you plant seed potatoes, give them a good head start by encouraging their shoots to begin sprouting. This simple process is known as chitting.

At the beginning of the month, place each seed potato into an egg box segment, making sure that the end with the most "eyes" (indented marks on the skin) points upwards. Put your potatoes somewhere light and cool, perhaps a porch. Within a couple of weeks, sturdy green shoots will emerge from the eyes. Ideally the shoots will be 2–4cm (1–1½in) long by the second half of March, when the weather should be getting warm enough for planting.

1. There is space for two rows of four potato plants in your raised bed. Create the first row down the middle of section one (15cm/6in from the short edge of the bed) and another down the middle of section two (30cm/1ft on from the first). Lay your first seed potato on the soil about 15cm (6in) from the long edge of the bed, and then space them 30cm (1ft) apart along the rows.

2. Lift each seed potato and use a trowel to dig a hole 20cm (8in) deep under its position. Gently drop the seed potato into the hole, with the end with the most sprouts facing skywards.

3. If the soil is dry, water each potato by pouring about 500ml (16fl oz) of water into the planting hole, but if the soil is already moist this isn't necessary. Backfill soil into the hole with your hand or a trowel. Label your rows to mark their location and remind you which variety you are growing.

SHORT, STURDY SHOOTS
Encouraging seed potatoes into growth before planting gets them off to the best start.

SEED POTATOES SOLD IN GARDEN CENTRES MAY ALREADY HAVE STARTED SPROUTING. THIS CAN BE AN EASY WAY TO MAKE UP SOME TIME, BUT BE CAREFUL NOT TO DAMAGE THE SHOOTS WHEN REMOVING THE POTATOES FROM THE PACKAGING.

APRIL

BEST THING ABOUT APRIL
Transplanting broad beans
and seeing potatoes appear

WORST THING ABOUT APRIL
It usually goes by too quickly

WATCH OUT FOR IN APRIL
Still a strong chance of frost
for many areas of the UK

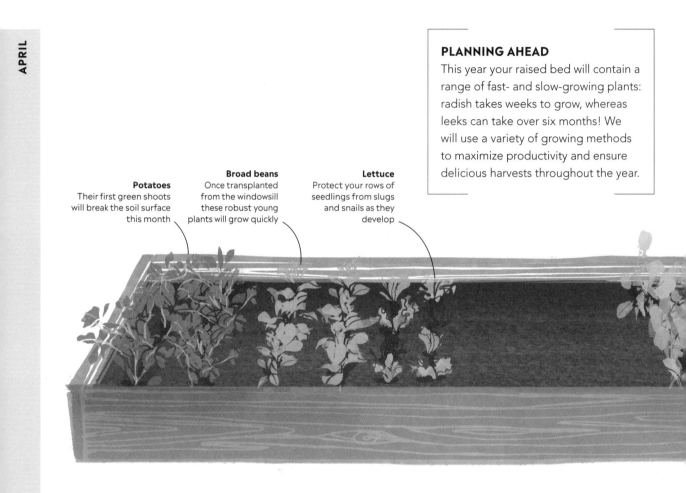

PLANNING AHEAD
This year your raised bed will contain a range of fast- and slow-growing plants: radish takes weeks to grow, whereas leeks can take over six months! We will use a variety of growing methods to maximize productivity and ensure delicious harvests throughout the year.

Potatoes
Their first green shoots will break the soil surface this month

Broad beans
Once transplanted from the windowsill these robust young plants will grow quickly

Lettuce
Protect your rows of seedlings from slugs and snails as they develop

APRIL
AT A GLANCE

Thanks to April's rising temperatures, it's "all systems go" in the raised bed and many vegetables can now be planted outside. Be cautious though, as there may still be frosts at night in temperate areas. Frost-hardy crops will be fine, but tender potato shoots need protection on cold nights.

HOW THE BED WILL LOOK
This is the month when your bed will begin to turn green. Newly transplanted broad beans make an instant impact, while radish and lettuce seedlings will both grow rapidly. Clusters of potato shoots will also appear in April.

Potatoes
2 rows

Lettuce
2 rows

ON THE PLAN
Half of the bed is already satisfyingly full of crops. The rest remains empty, waiting for later sowings and the crops from the windowsill.

KEY

Empty

Transplant

Grow on

Harvest

1   Section number

Broad beans
2 rows

Empty

Radish
2 rows

Radishes
Pick your first brightly coloured radishes from the bed in mid-April

ON THE WINDOWSILL
Start off
• Sow leek seeds into a deep pot and germinate them on a warm windowsill.
• Sow runner beans into deep modules and keep them warm and moist.

Grow on
• Water your broad beans regularly to keep the compost moist until they are planted out later this month.

IN THE RAISED BED
Grow on
• Transplant your broad beans into sections three and four after briefly hardening the plants off.
• Protect the new leaves of potato plants if frost is forecast by covering them with fleece or cardboard.
• Protect your lettuce seedlings from slugs and snails, and try thinning the plants in one row to about 15cm (6in) apart.

Harvest
• Pull the first radishes from the soil when their roots are about 2.5cm (1in) in diameter.

MAINTENANCE CHECKLIST
• Water.
• Weed.
• Harden off.
• Protect young plants from pests.

ON YOUR WINDOWSILL

The windowsill becomes a production line for a range of seedlings in April.
Your broad beans will be ready to transplant from the middle of the month,
but share the space for now with newly sown runner beans and leeks.

START OFF
LEEKS

SEED TO TRANSPLANT
10–12 weeks

POSITION
Sunny windowsill

WATER
Every 3–4 days

TRANSPLANT
June

HARVEST
Winter

HUW'S TOP VARIETIES
'Bandit'
'Blue Green Autumn'
'Musselburgh'

Leeks are a hardy but slow-growing crop, which means that although they are a staple vegetable during winter, they need to be sown now. Their spindly seedlings are tougher than they look and leeks can be sown outdoors, but if grown in small quantities, I like to cosset them on the windowsill to ensure good germination and eliminate the need for fiddly weeding. The young plants will be ready to be planted into their final positions in June. I always grow leeks because there's something deeply reassuring about knowing that they will be there to harvest on a bleak January day for a warming winter soup.

SOWING LEEKS

I like to sow my leeks in the first week of April. The tiny seeds can all be sown into the same pot and grown on together as seedlings. This means they will need a pot that is 10cm (4in) wide, and at least 8cm (3in) deep, to allow them space to develop. Find them a sunny spot on the windowsill and the slender, grass-like seedlings will unfurl from the soil after about two weeks.

If space becomes tight on the windowsill, move the whole pot of seedlings into the bed once they are 5cm (2in) tall. Sink the pot into the soil between where the runner beans and row of beetroot will be planted (*see diagram, p85*). The leeks can then be lifted and transplanted in June (*see pp90–91*).

1

2

3

ANOTHER OPTION IS TO RAISE LEEK SEEDLINGS OUTDOORS. SOW SEED THICKLY ALONG A 60CM (2FT) LONG ROW, AND THIN SEEDLINGS TO 2.5CM (1IN) APART. TRANSPLANT IN JUNE.

1. Fill a 10cm (4in) wide pot that is at least 8cm (3in) deep with multi-purpose compost, to about 2.5cm (1in) below its rim.

2. Sprinkle at least 20 seeds thinly over the surface of the compost using your thumb and forefinger.

3. Cover the seeds with about 1cm (½in) of compost, and water thoroughly. Allow the pot to drain well before placing it on a warm, sunny windowsill.

55

START OFF

RUNNER BEANS

SEED TO TRANSPLANT
6–8 weeks

POSITION
Warm, sunny windowsill

WATER
Every 2–3 days

TRANSPLANT
End of May

HARVEST
August

HUW'S TOP VARIETIES
'Enorma'
'Prizewinner'
'Scarlet Emperor'

Runner beans are decorative as well as a productive vegetable, because their height adds structure to the garden, they have amazing scarlet flowers, and their long pods taste wonderful. They are easy to grow, but because they are a tender vegetable, they need warmth to germinate and protection from frost. You can provide this, and give them an early start, by sowing them indoors in mid-April, before transplanting them into the raised bed once the weather is milder in late spring. They will then produce a plentiful harvest of delicious pods right through August and September.

SOW RUNNER BEANS

Runner bean seeds are large and root deeply, so they are best planted in the cardboard tubes from the centre of loo

rolls, trays of deep modules, or special containers called root trainers (shown here). They germinate reliably, so you only need to plant one bean per pot. There will be space for eight runner bean plants in the raised bed, but sow around 14 seeds in case of any failures and to allow you to select the strongest plants. Heat is required for germination, so place the pots in a warm, sunny position after sowing. Keep the compost moist but not waterlogged, and seedlings should appear in around seven to ten days.

1

2

CROP SWAP

If you don't like runner beans, you could try growing Borlotti climbing French beans instead, using the same instructions. Sow seed in April, transplant in May, and the beans will be ready to harvest in August.

1. Fill your planting containers to the top with multi-purpose compost without compacting it at all. Then place a seed on top and press it down about 2cm (¾in) into the compost with your finger. Sow seeds in 14 modules.

2. Fill in the hole above each seed with compost, being careful not to miss any.

3. Remove any excess compost from the surface of the containers with your hand. Water thoroughly and allow the water to drain. Place the tray on a sunny windowsill and keep the compost moist.

3

GROW ON
BROAD BEANS

These young plants should now be growing rapidly. Make sure that they don't dry out by watering every two days and checking their pots regularly to ensure that they don't need more. Turn the pots daily on the windowsill to prevent the plants growing towards the light. In early April start to acclimatize them to outdoor conditions, or "harden off" (*see p13*). Do this by moving them outdoors during the day for three consecutive days and bringing them in at night. They will then be ready to transplant on the fourth day.

BROAD BEANS ARE HARDY PLANTS, GOOD AT ADAPTING TO TEMPERATURE CHANGE, SO THEY DON'T NEED TO BE HARDENED OFF FOR LONG BEFORE MAKING THE MOVE FROM WINDOWSILL TO RAISED BED.

IN YOUR

RAISED BED

The raised bed comes alive this month, with broad beans transplanted from the windowsill instantly filling two rows. All of your young plants will be particularly vulnerable to pests, so protect them from slugs and birds.

GROW ON

BROAD BEANS

**TRANSPLANT
TO HARVEST**
10–11 weeks

LIGHT
Full sun

**PLANTING
DISTANCE**
20cm (8in) apart

HARDINESS
Fully hardy

KEY PROBLEMS
Blackfly
Rust

HARVEST
July

TRANSPLANTING INTO THE BED

When your broad beans are about 10cm (4in) tall, they are ready for transplanting once they have been hardened off. The plants may have sent out a long tap root from the base of the cardboard tube, which needs to be handled carefully. If this tap root snaps during transplanting, the plant's development can be slightly affected.

Begin to harden off your broad bean plants at the beginning of April, by putting them outside during the day for three days. Give them a thorough watering before transplanting them into the raised bed. Transplant a row of broad bean plants into section three, and a row into section four.

1

1. Use a ruler to measure 30cm (1ft) from the row of potatoes in section two, and mark your first row of broad beans by laying a cane across the width of the bed. Mark the second row 30cm (1ft) from the first. About 10cm (4in) from the bed's long edge, use a trowel to dig a hole in the first row, just deeper and wider than the roots of the plant.

2. Carefully place the plant into the hole, so that the soil is at the same level on the plant's stem as the compost in the pot. If the plants are growing in cardboard tubes, plant those too.

3. Push the soil around the base of the seedling to firm it in and then water it thoroughly. Plant six seedlings in each row in the same way, spacing them 20cm (8in) apart along the rows.

USING CARDBOARD TUBES MEANS THAT THERE IS VERY LITTLE DISTURBANCE OR DAMAGE TO ROOTS WHEN YOUNG PLANTS ARE PLANTED OUT INTO THE RAISED BED.

2

3

WEEDING

Follow a few simple tips and weeds will never be a problem in your raised bed. The two best pieces of news are:

• A single raised bed is a small and simple space to manage weeds.
• Weeding is easy once you've learned to recognize what needs to be removed (*see pp216–217*).

Be vigilant and remove weeds while they are just seedlings. This stops them developing a strong root system, when they become harder to remove. Many people like to hoe weeds, which is effective in the short term, but can expose buried weed seeds and entice them to germinate, meaning another generation of weeds. Mulching and covering the soil in winter are also good ways to prevent weed growth.

KEEP AN EYE OUT
Watch for weeds while you get on with other tasks: as soon as you see a weed pull it out!

GROW ON
POTATOES

As they push their shoots through the soil, the only help potatoes need is protection from frost. Check the weather forecast and cover the row with horticultural fleece or cardboard if the temperature is set to fall below 4°C (39°F). Don't panic, though; plants will recover from damage caused by a light frost and send up fresh new shoots.

FROST PROTECTION
Lay a covering of horticultural fleece over your potato plants to protect them from frost.

GROW ON
LETTUCE

You can thin out your lettuce seedlings, but it's not essential, because plants grown densely will thrive as long as you harvest from them regularly. Try thinning one row and leaving the other to see the difference. Remove weaker plants with scissors to leave plants spaced 15cm (6in) apart. Add the thinnings to your salads.

HARVEST
RADISH

The vibrant, crisp roots of your radishes are the first home-grown crop from your raised bed. Their lovely crunch and peppery heat are just a taste of what's to come!

HOW TO HARVEST
Start looking to see if your radishes are ready for picking from late April, by pulling aside the leaves to check the size of the roots (*see opposite*). If the top of the root is about 2cm (¾in) wide, then it is ready to harvest. Gently pull the base of the leaves and the root will come out of the soil. Pick larger roots first, leaving the smaller ones to grow on. Wash and eat them as soon as possible after picking.

MAY

BEST THING ABOUT MAY
You can transplant your
tender vegetables outdoors

WORST THING ABOUT MAY
Young plants often require lots of
watering while they get established

WATCH OUT FOR IN MAY
Late frosts can damage or
kill tender vegetable plants.

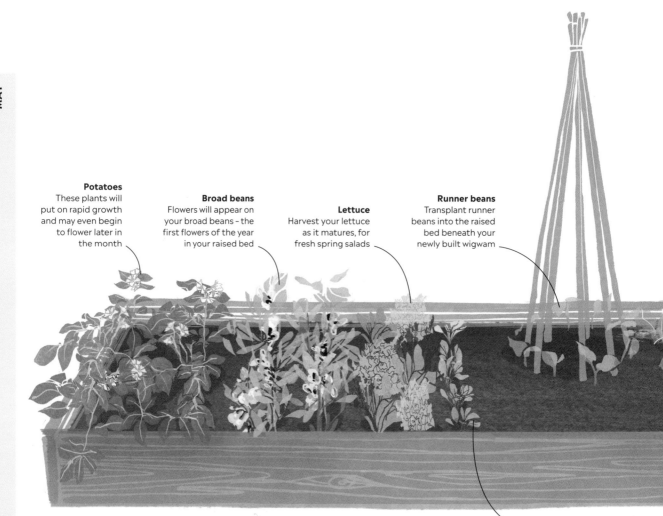

Potatoes
These plants will put on rapid growth and may even begin to flower later in the month

Broad beans
Flowers will appear on your broad beans – the first flowers of the year in your raised bed

Lettuce
Harvest your lettuce as it matures, for fresh spring salads

Runner beans
Transplant runner beans into the raised bed beneath your newly built wigwam

Swiss chard
Seedlings should start to appear in the bed a week or so after sowing

MAY
AT A GLANCE

May is perhaps my favourite month, because warmer weather spurs plants into lush growth and fruit trees into blossom. Late frosts are still a danger however, so be patient and wait for them to pass before transplanting vegetables that are sensitive to the cold, such as runner beans.

HOW YOUR BED WILL LOOK
By the end of May, your raised bed will be starting to look quite full, although most of the plants will still have plenty of growing to do.

ON THE PLAN
Runner beans and Swiss chard take up their spaces now. By the end of May, you will be harvesting lettuce as well as your radishes.

KEY

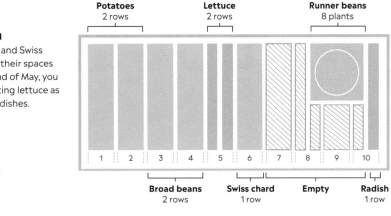

Potatoes
2 rows

Lettuce
2 rows

Runner beans
8 plants

Broad beans
2 rows

Swiss chard
1 row

Empty

Radish
1 row

▨	Empty
▨	Start off
▨	Transplant
▨	Grow on
▨	Harvest
1	Section number

Radishes
Any remaining radishes will be ready to pick over the course of the month

ON THE WINDOWSILL
Start off
• Sow dwarf French beans into individual pots and keep them warm.
• Pot up kale seedlings and keep them on the windowsill to develop.

Grow on
• Water your runner beans regularly, and make sure to harden them off before they are planted outdoors later in May.
• Turn and water your young leeks as they continue to grow slowly.

IN THE RAISED BED
Start off
• Sow Swiss chard seeds directly into the soil of the raised bed in section six. Thin them out once the seedlings appear.

Grow on
• Transplant your runner beans into the bed after the last frost. Build a wigwam to support them as they grow.
• Earth up your potatoes to encourage the tubers to grow, and use horticultural fleece to protect them from the cold on frosty nights.
• Add bamboo canes to support your broad beans in windy weather.
• Protect your lettuce from slugs and snails.
• Water your radishes to ensure that they don't flower (and become bitter-tasting) before they are ready to be harvested.

Harvest
• Pick the outer leaves from your lettuces to enjoy a fresh harvest while keeping each plant cropping for longer.
• Continue to pull up your radishes once the tops of the colourful roots peep above the soil and reach about 2.5cm (1in) across. Sow another row when they are finished.

MAINTENANCE CHECKLIST
• Water.
• Weed.
• Keep the bed covered with netting to prevent birds damaging crops.
• Compost waste materials, such as the leaves from your harvested radishes, by adding them to your compost pile.

65

ON YOUR WINDOWSILL

May is a busy time on the windowsill. Pot up bought-in kale seedlings and sow dwarf French beans now, to grow alongside last month's sowings of leeks and runner beans.

START OFF

DWARF FRENCH BEANS

SEED TO TRANSPLANT
4–6 weeks

POSITION
Warm, sunny windowsill

WATER
Every 2–3 days

TRANSPLANT
June

HARVEST
August

HUW'S TOP VARIETIES
'Domino'
'Purple Teepee'
'The Prince'

Dwarf French beans are compact plants that are easy to grow and produce a prolific harvest. They don't need much attention once planted, and even cope well with periods of dry weather. They do require warmth to germinate, however, and will not survive frost once planted out.

SOWING DWARF FRENCH BEANS

These large seeds are easy to handle and sow, and don't root as deeply as other beans, so you can use standard pots or modules. Old yogurt pots or washing-up liquid bottles work well as pots, or you could use cardboard toilet roll tubes like those used to sow broad beans (*see p40*). Warmth is needed for germination, so place the pots in a cosy, sunny spot after sowing; cold, wet conditions will cause the seeds to rot. Seedlings should appear in seven to ten days.

1. Carefully make several drainage holes in the base of each pot, using the tip of a sharp knife or a bradawl.

2. Fill each pot to about 1cm (½in) below the rim with multi-purpose compost. Not filling to the top makes watering easier.

3. Push one seed about 5cm (2in) deep into the centre of each pot with your finger. Water the pots thoroughly, let them drain well, and place them on your windowsill. Keep them moist, but not soaked, by watering every three days, or every two days in warm weather.

START OFF
KALE

SEEDLING TO TRANSPLANT
8–10 weeks

POSITION
Cool, partial shade

WATER
Every 2–3 days

TRANSPLANT
July

HARVEST
November onwards

HUW'S TOP VARIETIES
'Dwarf Blue Curled Scotch'
'Nero di Toscana'
'Red Winter'

Plants from the cabbage family grow well in temperate climates, and hardy kale is particularly suitable for lower temperatures. If you start seedlings on the windowsill in May, you'll be able to plant them out in July, ready for harvesting as delicious greens right through winter.

START WITH SEEDLINGS

Just eight kale plants will give you plentiful pickings. Start with seedlings, as these are a reliable alternative to seed and don't cost much more to buy. Plant seedlings into individual pots to give them space to grow, and transplant them into your bed in July.

If you can't find seedlings to buy, start from seed, sowing three seeds into each of eight small pots. Remove the weaker seedlings when they reach 2.5cm (1in) high, and transplant them into the bed once you have harvested your broad beans.

1

2

3

1. Remove the seedlings from the tray in which you bought them. Gently separate them, prising apart each plant's roots. Be careful not to damage the roots when pulling seedlings apart.

2. Cover the base of a small pot with multi-purpose compost, put the seedling on top, and fill around the roots with compost. Top up the pot with compost, burying the stem up to the first side shoot where a leaf grows from the stem. This helps to support the plant.

3. Water the seedlings thoroughly and place them on a cool windowsill. Kale is hardy, so you can put them outside if there is no windowsill space.

CROP SWAP

If you don't like kale, you can grow red cabbage or purple sprouting broccoli instead, using the same instructions. Buy young plants or sow seed in May, transplant into your bed in July, and harvest from November, depending on the variety.

GROW ON
RUNNER BEANS

Keep your frost-tender runner beans inside until mid to late May, to avoid late frosts. The plants need to be toughened up (or "hardened off") for the outdoors before transplanting (*see p13*).

GROW ON
LEEKS

Water your seedlings every two to three days. Although their growth will be quite slow, they should gradually become taller and thicker. Turn them every day to prevent seedlings growing in one direction towards the light from the window.

IN YOUR

RAISED BED

The bed begins to fill up as Swiss chard is sown and runner beans are planted out this month. Your potato plants will also require a little attention to encourage the best possible crop.

START OFF
SWISS CHARD

SEED TO HARVEST
8–16 weeks

LIGHT
Full sun or
partial shade

**PLANTING
DISTANCE**
25cm (10in)

HARDINESS
Fully hardy

KEY PROBLEMS
Birds
Slugs and snails
Downy Mildew

HARVEST
July to August

**HUW'S TOP
VARIETIES**
'Bright Lights' seed mix
'Magenta Sunset'
'Rhubarb Chard'

Also known as rainbow chard, this leafy vegetable adds an ornamental quality to your growing patch with its vibrantly coloured stems. Swiss chard germinates easily, and can be sown directly into the bed in mid-May. Protect the crop from bird damage by covering it with netting. The first leaves will be ready to harvest in July.

SOW DIRECTLY INTO THE BED

Swiss chard seeds are generally sown in late spring, because earlier sowings tend to bolt (flowering or running to seed prematurely), ruining the taste. When sowing, use a tape measure to mark the right distance between each sowing point or "station". Sow the seeds in a row down the middle of section six.

1

2

3

4

1. Extend a tape measure across the bed widthways, about 20cm (8in) from the nearest row of lettuces. This should be the middle of section six.

2. Starting 10cm (4in) away from the long edge of the bed, use your finger to create a hole in the soil 1cm (½in) deep every 25cm (10in).

3. Sow three to four seeds in each hole, remove the tape measure, cover the seeds with soil, and water well.

4. Seedlings should emerge within two weeks. Thin the seedlings by pinching out the stems of the weakest plants between your fingers until only the strongest one remains. Don't pull the seedlings up, as this may damage the roots of the remaining seedlings. The thinnings make a delicious addition to salads.

CROP SWAP

If you don't like Swiss chard, you can grow perpetual spinach instead, using the same instructions. Sow seed in May and it will be ready to harvest from July onwards.

GROW ON
RUNNER BEANS

**TRANSPLANT
TO HARVEST**
8–12 weeks

LIGHT
Full sun or
partial shade

**PLANTING
DISTANCE**
15cm (6in)

HARDINESS
Frost tender

KEY PROBLEMS
Aphids
Slugs and snails

HARVEST
August to September

Vigorous runner bean plants need a tall structure to support their climbing stems, particularly once they are laden with a heavy crop of pods. Build them a tall wigwam of bamboo canes, and transplant them into the soil at its base once all risk of frost has passed, which can be the end of May in cooler areas. The wigwam should be positioned 15cm (6in) from your radishes, and 8cm (3in) from the long side of your raised bed. The diameter of the wigwam should be about 45cm (1½ft).

TRANSPLANTING INTO THE BED
Once your runner beans are hardened off (*see p13*), they will be ready to transplant. Make sure you don't transplant your beans until two weeks after the average date of the last frost where you live.

1. If you grew your beans in plastic pots, gently remove a seedling from its pot; cardboard tubes can be left in place. Then dig a hole in the soil between two of the wigwam's supports. The hole should be deeper and wider than the roots of the seedling.

2. Put the seedling into the hole and align the top of its root ball so that it is level with the soil in the bed. Push soil into the hole around the roots and press gently with your fingers to firm the seedling in place. Repeat these steps for the remaining seedlings, planting one in each of the gaps between the wigwam's canes.

3. Finally, give the seedlings a good water to settle the soil around the roots as well as provide them with a drink. Aim for eight seconds per plant if you are using a watering can.

BUILD A WIGWAM
You can use any kind of sticks for this, as long as they are at least 2m (6½ft) long. I recommend using bamboo canes for ease and low cost.

1. Push eight bamboo sticks into the ground to form a circle with a diameter of around 45cm (1½ft). They should be about 30cm (1ft) deep in the soil.

2. Gather the tops of the sticks together and tie them securely by looping garden string around them several times and knotting it tightly.

73

TAKE YOUR TIME TO BUILD A STURDY
WIGWAM FOR YOUR RUNNER BEANS.
ITS HEIGHT WILL MAKE IT A PROMINENT
FEATURE IN YOUR GARDEN ONCE THE
PLANTS CLIMB THE CANES AND COVER
THEM WITH BRIGHT GREEN FOLIAGE AND
SPECTACULAR SCARLET FLOWERS.

GROW ON
POTATOES

Protect the young leaves of your potato plants from frost damage on cold nights (below 4°C/39°F) by covering them with horticultural fleece. When the shoots are are around 10cm (4in) tall, it's time for earthing up.

EARTH UP YOUR POTATOES

This simply means mounding earth up around the stems to encourage them upward. This increases the space for the potato tubers to grow and prevents them being exposed to light, which turns them green. Earth up using a rake when the soil is soft, ideally after rain.

1. Start with the rake around halfway between your two rows of potatoes and begin raking the earth up and around the stems along one row. Rake up as much earth as possible, so that no more can be added to the mound without it falling back down again.

2. Repeat the process with the other side of the row, and then set to work earthing up the second row. You should now have two rows of mounds with just the tips of your plants showing.

3. You can fill the "valleys" between the hills with grass clippings. These will act as a mulch to help retain moisture in the soil and suppress weeds.

THE NEXT TIME YOU WILL NEED TO TOUCH YOUR POTATOES AFTER EARTHING THEM UP IS IN JUNE, WHEN IT COMES TO HARVESTING THEM. LET ME TELL YOU, IT IS WORTH THE WAIT!

GROW ON

BROAD BEANS

Broad beans are tough plants and generally need little attention, but if your bed is a little exposed, or windy weather is forecast, they will benefit from some support as they grow (*top left*). Push a 60cm (2ft) long stick or bamboo cane about 30cm (1ft) into the soil 5cm (2in) from the stem of each plant.

Loosely tie the stem to the stick with string, so that your thumb fits between them – tying too tightly around the growing stem can choke the plant. If your broad beans are growing in a sheltered position, they will only need extra support if the weather is forecast to be particularly wet and windy.

GROW ON

LETTUCE

As your lettuces develop hearts and become ready to pick, make sure that slugs and snails don't get to their delicious leaves first. Watch out for slimy trails and holes in leaves, taking control measures if you spot signs of trouble. For example, try leaving out a grapefruit skin to trap them

(*top right*). Cut a grapefruit in half and hollow it out. Then cut two squares in from the edge on either side of each half, and leave in the bed. Check back the next morning to see if anything is hiding inside (*see p47 and p219 for more information on slugs and snails*).

GROW ON

RADISH

The vibrant roots of your radishes (*opposite*) should continue to swell, but will become tough and bitter if the plants start to "bolt" (send up flower stems). This is encouraged by dry conditions, so do water every couple of days if there is no rain.

Don't worry if a few of your plants do bolt, though, because if left they will develop fat, edible seed pods at the top of their stems, which will make a great alternative crop to harvest in June.

HARVEST
LETTUCE

Savour the juiciness and flavour of the first salad leaves freshly picked from your raised bed. They are a world away from shop-bought lettuce, and just a small taste of the many delicious crops to come!

HOW TO HARVEST

When your lettuce has a plump heart, or a generous rosette of leaves if it's a non-hearting variety, then you can start to harvest it. The best way to do this is to simply pick or cut the larger leaves from the outside of the plant as you need them (*see opposite*). This allows the growing point at the centre of the plant to keep producing new leaves, which will give you a steady supply of salad for several weeks. Picking in this way also means that you only harvest what you need, so nothing goes to waste.

HARVEST
RADISH

Continue to harvest your radishes when they reach a good size – about 2.5cm (1in) across. Be sure to eat them all by the end of May, before the roots toughen or start to taste too hot. Once they are all gone, re-sow a single row in the same spot for a harvest at the end of June. If you would prefer to try picking edible green seed pods, leave the last plants from your first sowing to flower, and harvest pods in June.

RETURNING RADISHES
Radish can be re-sown again and again, providing a quick harvest of roots within four weeks of sowing.

JUNE

BEST THING ABOUT JUNE
Plants grow rapidly as the weather warms

WORST THING ABOUT JUNE
Windy days can damage tall bean plants

WATCH OUT FOR IN JUNE
Insect pests, such as aphids,
also flourish in warm weather

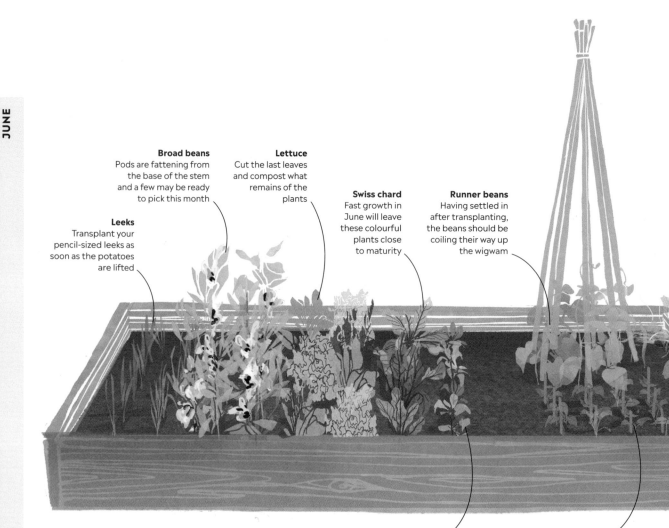

Broad beans
Pods are fattening from the base of the stem and a few may be ready to pick this month

Lettuce
Cut the last leaves and compost what remains of the plants

Swiss chard
Fast growth in June will leave these colourful plants close to maturity

Runner beans
Having settled in after transplanting, the beans should be coiling their way up the wigwam

Leeks
Transplant your pencil-sized leeks as soon as the potatoes are lifted

Beetroot
Tiny clusters of leaves will be visible one to two weeks after sowing

Dwarf French beans
Once established, these vigorous plants should be putting on bushy growth by the end of June

JUNE AT A GLANCE

June's greatest pleasure will be seeing your first harvest of new potatoes pop from the ground as you lift your fork. Frosts are now over for the summer, and a second batch of vegetables can be started once the earliest salad crops come to an end, making maximum use of the space in your bed.

HOW YOUR BED WILL LOOK
The bed gets increasingly colourful in June, as your maturing potatoes and broad beans attract insects with their flowers. Vibrant Swiss chard stems also add a burst of brightness in the centre of the bed as the plants grow taller and sturdier, alongside the new row of burgundy-veined beetroot seedlings.

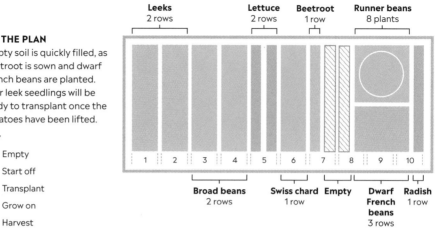

ON THE PLAN
Empty soil is quickly filled, as beetroot is sown and dwarf French beans are planted. Your leek seedlings will be ready to transplant once the potatoes have been lifted.

KEY

▨	Empty
▧	Start off
▧	Transplant
▧	Grow on
▧	Harvest
⦙ 1 ⦙	Section number

Leeks
2 rows

Lettuce
2 rows

Beetroot
1 row

Runner beans
8 plants

Broad beans
2 rows

Swiss chard
1 row

Empty

Dwarf French beans
3 rows

Radish
1 row

Radishes
Pick roots from your second sowing in May at the end of the month, or harvest edible seed pods

ON THE WINDOWSILL
Start off
• Sow peas into modules to transplant in July and pick from August. Starting peas indoors prevents mice eating the shoots.

Grow on
• Water leek seedlings to keep the compost moist.
• Harden off dwarf French beans to transplant into the bed later this month.
• Water kale regularly.

IN THE RAISED BED
Start off
• Sow knobbly beetroot seeds directly into the soil of section seven.

Grow on
• Transplant your leeks and dwarf French beans into the bed once hardened off.
• Train your runner beans up their supports by helping them to twist around the canes and tying their stems with garden twine.

• Look out for blight on your potatoes and chop down the stems if you spot any.
• Pinch out the top growth of broad bean plants to prevent blackfly infestation.
• Remove any Swiss chard leaves with brown patches – these indicate pests.

Harvest
• Unearth your new potatoes and enjoy them simply boiled with melted butter.
• Pop a few sweet baby broad beans from their pods at the end of the month.
• Pick the last of your lettuce leaves. Remove the plants from the bed and compost them once they are finished.
• Pull the second crop of crisp radishes.

MAINTENANCE CHECKLIST
• Water.
• Weed.
• Harden off plants before transplanting.
• Watch out for pests.
• Use netting to cover the bed and prevent birds from damaging crops.
• Compost waste and weeds.

ON YOUR

WINDOWSILL

The procession of seedlings continues on the windowsill in June. Peas grown for pods are newly sown, while sturdy young leek and dwarf French bean plants will be ready to plant out later in the month.

START OFF
PEAS

SEED TO TRANSPLANT
4–6 weeks

POSITION
Sunny windowsill

WATER
Every 2–3 days

TRANSPLANT
July

HARVEST
August

HUW'S TOP VARIETIES
Shelling: 'Meteor'
Sugar snap: 'Nairobi'
Mangetout:
'Oregon Sugar Pod'

Peas grown to maturity for their pods are a "must-have" vegetable. The sweetness of freshly picked peas is quite unlike those bought from a supermarket. Peas are easy to grow, but they need supporting twigs and a moist soil to produce a good crop. The three main types of peas are all grown in the same way. Shelling or English peas are popped from the pod and eaten; sugar snap peas have edible pods that are eaten with the fat peas inside; mangetout peas are eaten as flat, unripe pods. Dried peas work well for pea shoots, but will not produce the tastiest fresh peas. Choose

FRESHLY PICKED PEAS TASTE THE SWEETEST, SO EAT THEM UP QUICKLY! AS SOON AS YOU PICK PEAS THE SUGARS IN THEM BEGIN TURNING INTO STARCH, WHICH IS WHAT CHANGES THEIR FLAVOUR.

1

a named variety of garden peas instead: the dwarf pea variety 'Meteor' is a good choice for the limited space in the raised bed, because it only grows to a height of about 35cm (14in).

SOWING PEAS

Start off peas grown for pods indoors to keep them out of the reach of mice, which eat the seeds and nibble the new shoots outdoors. Peas don't root deeply and will grow well in newspaper pots (*see pp144– 145*), module trays from the garden centre, or even yogurt pots that have had drainage holes added.

2

3

1. Place multi-purpose compost into the modules and gently press it down to make sure that each module is properly filled to about 2.5cm (1in) below its rim.

2. Put three pea seeds on the compost in each module, push them down gently, and cover with 1cm (½in) of compost. Water thoroughly and place on a tray, but don't leave them standing in water. Put the tray on the windowsill. The following day, cover with a sheet of newspaper to retain moisture, and check underneath it every day for growth.

3. Once the peas sprout, usually in less than a week, remove the newspaper and water every two or three days.

GROW ON
LEEKS

Now that your seedlings are becoming taller and sturdier it is almost time to transplant them. Continue to water them every two or three days to ensure that the compost is kept moist as their expanding roots begin to fill the pot.

GROW ON
DWARF FRENCH BEANS

These tender plants are easily damaged by cold, windy weather, so it's important to harden them off and acclimatize them to outdoor conditions before transplanting them. Put them in a sheltered position outdoors for slightly longer each day for ten days, keeping them watered (see p13).

GROW ON
KALE

Keep watering your kale regularly and turn their pots to stop them growing towards the light. If space is tight on the windowsill, these hardy plants can be grown on outdoors before planting them out in July.

IN YOUR RAISED BED

The bed is bustling now, as established crops grow rapidly and newcomers are sown and transplanted. Maintaining the bed will only take about half an hour this month, though, excluding watering, so don't feel overwhelmed.

START OFF

BEETROOT

SEED TO HARVEST
10–16 weeks

LIGHT
Full sun or
partial shade

**PLANTING
DISTANCE**
Thin to 5cm
(2in) apart

HARDINESS
Moderately hardy

KEY PROBLEMS
Birds
Leaf miner
Slugs and snails

HARVEST
September
to October

**HUW'S TOP
VARIETIES**
'Boltardy'
'Cylindra'
'Rhonda'

Many people think they don't like beetroot until they taste the home-grown version. The wonderful earthy sweetness and smooth texture of the roots really don't need to be doused in vinegar. The leaves also make a great addition to salads when young, and look attractive in the raised bed with their dark red veins.

SOWING BEETROOT

The large seeds are easy to sow directly into the bed and will germinate reliably in one or two weeks. Most beetroot varieties are "multigerm" – in other words, what you sow is actually a cluster of several seeds and will produce more than one seedling. This means it's important to sow sparingly along the row and thin out the seedlings promptly to prevent overcrowding. Sow them alongside their relation Swiss chard in the raised bed, leaving around 15–20cm (6–8in) between the rows to allow enough space for both vegetables to develop.

1. Around 4–6 hours before sowing, soak the seeds in warm water. This will help to speed up germination.

2. Use string or a bamboo cane to mark out a straight line across the width of the bed, about 15–20cm (6–8in) from your row of Swiss chard. Use the handle of your rake to create a shallow trench 1–2cm (½–¾in) deep.

3. Remove the seeds from the water and sow them thinly along the line, leaving approximately 1cm (½in) between each seed.

4. Cover the seeds with soil using your hands or the back of the rake, and add a plant label to mark the row. Give the row a good water using a watering can with a rose attached. In dry weather, water the row well once every two days, even if the seedlings haven't appeared.

IN DRY WEATHER, WATER THE ROW WELL
ONCE EVERY TWO DAYS, EVEN BEFORE THE
SEEDLINGS HAVE APPEARED.

89

GROW ON

LEEKS

**TRANSPLANT
TO HARVEST**
17–27 weeks

LIGHT
Full sun

**PLANTING
DISTANCE**
15cm (6in) apart

HARDINESS
Fully hardy

KEY PROBLEMS
Slugs and snails
Rust

HARVEST
December
to March

Once the stems of your leeks are about 8mm (⅓in) in diameter, they will be ready to transplant out into their final growing positions. They will reach this size towards the end of the month, when you will have made space for them in the bed by lifting your crop of new potatoes.

TRANSPLANT INTO THE BED
To prepare for planting, simply level the surface of the soil in sections one and two with a rake. If your pot of seedlings has been growing in the raised bed, dig it up. The seedlings then need to be separated before they are transplanted.

NOT BACKFILLING THE LEEK'S PLANTING HOLE MEANS THERE IS LESS RESISTANCE WHEN THE STEM SWELLS, HOPEFULLY RESULTING IN FATTER LEEKS!

1. Remove the seedlings from the pot: turn the pot upside down, supporting the soil with your hand, and tap the base until the seedlings and compost fall free. Place the root ball in a bucket of water for 10 minutes to loosen the compost, and then tease the seedlings' roots apart. Put the 12 best seedlings in water to prevent the roots from drying out.

2. Mark out two rows across the width of the bed with string or canes, one down the middle of section one (15cm/6in from the short end of the bed) and the second down the middle of section two (30cm/1ft away from the first). Use a dibber or your rake handle to create holes around 15–20cm (6–8in) deep at 15cm (6in) intervals along the rows.

3. Carefully drop a leek seedling into each hole, gently poking down any roots that get stuck.

4. Pour water into each hole for five seconds. This will knock soil down to cover the roots and firm the plant in. Don't add any more soil to the hole.

GROW ON

DWARF FRENCH BEANS

**TRANSPLANT
TO HARVEST**
8–10 weeks

LIGHT
Full sun

**PLANTING
DISTANCE**
10cm (4in) apart

HARDINESS
Frost tender

KEY PROBLEMS
Aphids
Birds
Slugs and snails

HARVEST
August to September

Your dwarf French bean plants will be ready for transplanting around the midpoint of the month, once they are hardened off. They can take a week or two to settle into their new home, so don't worry if they don't romp away immediately after transplanting.

TRANSPLANT INTO THE BED

Twelve dwarf bean plants should fit into the empty square next to the runner beans. Mark out three rows, with the first 30cm (1ft) from the short end of the bed, and the next two 15cm (6in) and 30cm (1ft) after that. Within each row, plant four seedlings spaced 12cm (4¾in) apart.

1. Water the plants thoroughly before carefully removing the first seedling from its pot. Dig a hole a little deeper than the root ball of the seedling using a trowel or your hand.

2. Place the plant into the hole, so that the top of its root ball is level with the soil surface, and firm the soil around the stem with your fingers. Repeat for the remaining plants.

3. Add support to keep the seedlings upright by pushing short canes into the soil next to their stems and tying them in loosely with string.

4. If the soil is dry, water each plant for ten seconds using a watering can fitted with a rose. If the soil is already moist, water for only five seconds.

1

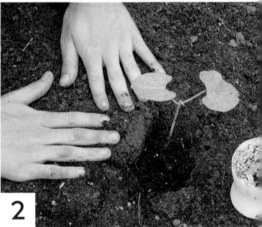

2

**KEEP AN EYE ON THE WEATHER
FORECAST AND SAVE YOURSELF
SOME WATERING BY SOWING SEEDS
AND TRANSPLANTING SEEDLINGS
WHEN IT'S JUST ABOUT TO RAIN.**

3

4

GROW ON
RUNNER BEANS

Once the plants are established, the long stems of your runner beans will be twining around the canes of their wigwam to climb rapidly. Help them along by training them when necessary and watering them regularly in dry weather.

Training runner beans is a simple but important task, because sometimes runner bean plants do not grow up their supports as intended. They may also be dislodged by windy weather. If you see a shoot trailing along the ground or flapping in the breeze, then gently hold it near the tip and wrap the stem around the desired bamboo cane. Check to see which way the stem is twisting and coil it around the cane in the same direction. It may stay there by itself, but to make sure, gently tie it in place with garden twine to keep it heading in the right direction.

IN TRAINING
The soft tips of runner bean stems snap easily, so be gentle when tying them in.

93

GROW ON

POTATOES

Your plants should now be fully grown, topped with flowers, and will be ready to harvest at the end of the month. If the weather is hot and dry, give the soil around them a really good soak once a week. This will help the developing potatoes to swell and increase your crop. Watch out for any potatoes poking through the soil surface and cover them up quickly to prevent the light turning them green, which makes them inedible.

FLOWERING TIME

Once the attractive white or purple flowers of your potato plants are fully open, it's worth checking around the roots to see if the soil holds new potatoes that are ready to harvest.

POTATO BLIGHT

This fungal disease affects both the leaves and potato tubers, causing them to rot. Warm, humid weather in July and August favours its spread, so your "first earlies", harvested in June, are at less risk than later "maincrops". If you see dark spots on leaves or brown lesions on stems, cut the stems to soil level with a sharp knife, and bin or burn them. Harvest any potatoes in the soil and eat them immediately.

GROW ON
BROAD BEANS

Now tall, flowering, and with their first pods forming, these plants don't need much attention this month, apart from taking a minute to cut off the top 8cm (3in) of stem at each plant's growing tip. This will prevent blackfly infesting the new shoots with their succulent young leaves, which you can enjoy eating instead.

BEAT THE PESTS
Eat delicious broad bean tops steamed or stir-fried.

GROW ON
SWISS CHARD

The large leaves and colourful stems of these plants should now look spectacular in your raised bed. Pick off any leaves that have more than 50 per cent of their surface covered by brown patches, these are caused by leaf mining insects (*see p219*). Water during hot, dry weather.

HARVEST
POTATOES

Unearthing your first potatoes is the most exciting harvest yet! Start in the second half of June, when plants are in flower. Dig around the roots with your hands to check if the potatoes are big enough to harvest.

HOW TO HARVEST
Place the fork about 30cm (1ft) away from the stem of the plant, to avoid damaging any potatoes. Push it down as far as it will go and press on the handle to gently lever the roots out of the ground. Lift the plant by its stem and the potatoes will pop from the soil. Check through the soil with your hands to find any that remain (*see opposite*). Wash and cook immediately, or leave the potatoes to dry in the sun for 6–8 hours before storing them in a dark, cool place.

HARVEST
BROAD BEANS

If you're lucky, there may be some early broad beans ready towards the end of June. Pick the first pods when they are about the length of a pencil. Pop out a few of the baby beans to experience their raw flavour – not too many as raw beans can cause an upset stomach – and save plenty to grow on for your main crop.

CONTINUE TO HARVEST
LETTUCE AND RADISHES

Check for pest damage and continue watering to keep your lettuce going. Pick the last leaves in early June, before the plants grow upwards to flower and become bitter. Uproot and compost spent plants.

You will also harvest the last of your radish roots or green, peppery seed pods at the end of the month, clearing the row so that your pea seedlings can be transplanted into that part of the bed during July.

JULY

BEST THING ABOUT JULY
Long warm summer evenings are
perfect for pottering in the garden

WORST THING ABOUT JULY
Hot, dry weather means that a
lot of watering is often needed

WATCH OUT FOR IN JULY
Slugs are active at night and can
wipe out vulnerable young plants

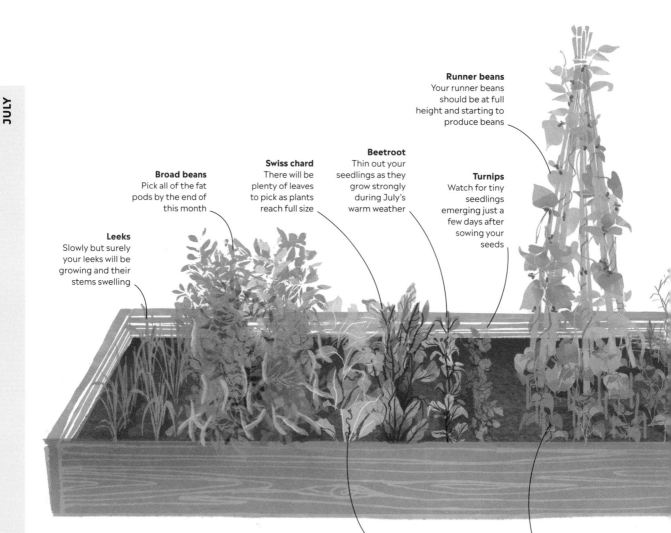

Runner beans
Your runner beans should be at full height and starting to produce beans

Beetroot
Thin out your seedlings as they grow strongly during July's warm weather

Turnips
Watch for tiny seedlings emerging just a few days after sowing your seeds

Swiss chard
There will be plenty of leaves to pick as plants reach full size

Broad beans
Pick all of the fat pods by the end of this month

Leeks
Slowly but surely your leeks will be growing and their stems swelling

Radishes
Sow seeds at the beginning of the month to harvest in early August

Dwarf French beans
Late July often brings the first slender pods, but your main crop will be in August

JULY
AT A GLANCE

July is a fantastic month for growth, and well-watered plants will develop incredibly quickly in hot summer weather. Long evenings will give you more time to tend your bed and get peas, turnips, and kale into the soil. There will be lots to harvest from your Swiss chard and broad beans, too.

HOW THE BED WILL LOOK
Mature rows of broad bean and Swiss chard plants dominate the bed at the start of the month. Runner beans and peas will quickly scale their supports in the summer warmth, and the dwarf French beans will bush out by the end of July. Your beetroot and turnips will also develop rapidly.

ON THE PLAN

Peas fill the gap left by the radishes, and the newly sown turnips will quickly germinate next to the beetroot. Broad beans and Swiss chard will be ready to harvest.

KEY

Empty

Start off

Transplant

Grow on

Harvest

1 : Section number

Peas
Once transplanted, your seedlings will quickly begin growing up their supports

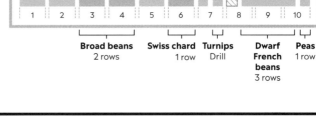

Leeks
2 rows

Radishes
2 rows

Beetroot
1 row

Empty

Runner beans
8 plants

Broad beans
2 rows

Swiss chard
1 row

Turnips
Drill

Dwarf French beans
3 rows

Peas
1 row

ON THE WINDOWSILL

Start off

• Sow winter lettuce into a seed tray to start off on the windowsill.

Grow on

• Prick out your winter lettuce seedlings into individual modules to grow on.

• Keep your peas and kale watered before they are transplanted later in July. Harden off your peas the week before transplanting.

IN THE BED

Start off

• Sow fast-growing turnips directly into half of section seven for a quick crop.

• Sow some more radish at the beginning of the month to fill space in section five.

Grow on

• Transplant your peas into half of section ten, adding branches to support them.

• Transplant your kale into sections three and four once the broad beans have been harvested and cleared from the bed.

• Water broad beans, Swiss chard and leeks during hot, dry weather.

• Thin out your turnip and beetroot seedlings to give them space to develop.

• Continue to tie in your runner beans to their supports. "Stop" the plants by pinching out their growing tips at the top of the wigwam.

• Stake dwarf French bean plants that need extra support because of the weight of their pods.

Harvest

• Pick the first outer leaves of your Swiss chard to enjoy steamed or stir-fried.

• Harvest the pods from your broad beans while they are small and sweet. Freeze any that you can't eat fresh.

MAINTENANCE CHECKLIST

• Weed.

• Water.

• Compost waste.

• Keep watch for pests and diseases.

• Harden off seedlings.

ON YOUR WINDOWSILL

The number of crops on the windowsill starts to fall in July, but a new sowing of winter lettuce will keep the supply of young plants coming as your kale and peas move outdoors to fill the raised bed.

START OFF

WINTER LETTUCE

SEED TO TRANSPLANT
4–6 weeks

POSITION
Cool site in full sun or partial shade

WATER
When the surface of the compost dries out

TRANSPLANT
August

HARVEST
September

HUW'S TOP VARIETIES
'May King'
'Veneziana'
'Winter Density'

Although called "winter" lettuce, these varieties only crop during winter if they are kept in a greenhouse. The name is given because, unlike many varieties of lettuce, they will survive in the ground over winter, and provide an early crop of leaves in spring when the weather thaws. The sowings you make now will provide a useful harvest through autumn, until the weather turns cold and light levels drop.

All varieties of lettuce will work as an autumn crop, so don't worry if you can't find winter lettuce. However, do use winter varieties if you can, as these have been bred to cope with colder weather.

SOWING WINTER LETTUCE

All you will need is a single packet of lettuce seeds, multi-purpose compost, and a seed tray (an old ice-cream or butter tub with drainage holes pierced in the base also works well). Always use fresh lettuce seed, because it germinates faster and more reliably than old seed.

As you are sowing the seeds in a single container, you will need to separate them out into individual pots later in the month so that they have space to develop (*see pp104–105*).

IF YOU LIVE IN A MILD AREA, YOU CAN ALSO SOW LETTUCE DIRECTLY INTO THE RAISED BED BETWEEN THE CHARD AND KALE ROWS. CREATE A 1CM (½IN) DEEP DRILL AND SOW SEEDS THICKLY AND EVENLY TO PRODUCE A DENSE ROW OF PLANTS.

1. Add a layer of compost at least 5cm (2in) deep to the base of the container, and level the surface gently with your hand. Sprinkle the lettuce seeds thinly and evenly over the compost using your thumb and forefinger.

2. Cover the seeds lightly with a layer of compost ½cm (¼in) deep. Lettuce seeds do not germinate well when buried deeply in the soil.

3. Water the tray thoroughly using your watering bottle with smaller holes. Place the seed tray on the windowsill and cover it with newspaper, to prevent the compost from drying out. Check daily and remove the newspaper when you notice the first seedlings coming through. There is no need to water the compost before this stage.

1

GROW ON

WINTER LETTUCE

Once your seedlings have two large leaves with a new shoot visible between them, it's time to gently lift them out of their seed tray and transplant them into a tray of small individual containers, known as modules. This is called "pricking out". Although it's a delicate process, you'll soon find a good rhythm. When handling any seedling, always hold it by a leaf, because it can survive a torn leaf, but a damaged stem will be fatal.

PRICK OUT YOUR SEEDLINGS

You will need a tray made up of small modules, and a pencil or plant label to prise the plants from their tray. There will be plenty of spare seedlings, so don't worry if you damage a few. Plant some undamaged spares into a container (see pp214–215).

1. Put a thin layer of multi-purpose compost into the base of the modules. Then take the seed tray containing your seedlings and carefully push the plant label into the compost. Use the label to start pushing seedlings out of the compost, gently freeing up their roots.

2. Take a seedling leaf between your thumb and index finger and gently pull it away from the others, using the plant label to tease apart any roots that are still stuck, but being careful to cause as little root damage as possible.

3. Place the seedling's roots into one of the modules, and fill around them with compost. Bury most of the stem to hold the plant firm, leaving the very top of the stem proud of the compost. Repeat until you have pricked out about 20 seedlings. Water gently using the watering bottle, and place the newly transplanted seedlings back on the windowsill.

2

3

KALE

Your kale should be making good growth in its pots on the windowsill. Water the seedlings every three to four days to ensure that the compost doesn't dry out.

GROW ON

PEAS

Water your pea seedlings every two to three days, never allowing their compost to dry out, and turn the pots 180 degrees once a day to prevent the plants bending towards the light. Keep them on the windowsill until they are 8–10cm (3–4in) tall, and then harden off the seedlings for a day or two before transplanting (*see p13*).

IN YOUR RAISED BED

*The bed is reaching its summer peak, with broad beans and Swiss chard
ready for picking and other vegetables rapidly maturing. Peas and kale
are transplanted and turnips sown, keeping the succession of crops coming.*

START OFF
TURNIPS

SEED TO HARVEST
6–10 weeks

LIGHT
Full sun, but can
manage partial shade

SOWING DISTANCE
1cm (½in)

HARDINESS
Moderately hardy

KEY PROBLEMS
Cabbage root fly
Flea beetle
Clubroot
Powdery mildew

HARVEST
September

**HUW'S TOP
VARIETIES**
'Purple Top Milan'
'Snowball'
'Sweet Bell'

Give home-grown turnips a chance,
because they are easy to grow, surprisingly
quick to mature, and the perfect crop for
filling any empty patches. They germinate
easily when sown directly into warm
summer soil and will need little care before
they are ready to harvest in September.

SOW DIRECTLY INTO THE BED
The easiest and most space-efficient way
to sow turnips is in a wide drill across the
width of the raised bed, which makes room
for more plants than a single row. They will
only take up half a section, so sow them in
section seven next to your beetroots.

1. Create a 1–2.5cm (½–1in) deep drill
across the width of the bed using
the handle of a rake or a stick of a
similar thickness.

2. Sow the seeds along the base of
the drill, across its full width, using
your thumb and forefinger. Turnip
seeds are relatively easy to handle,
so it should be simple to sow them
1cm (½in) apart.

3. Cover over with soil using your
hands or the rake, and label the
row. If there is no rain forecast
or the soil is dry, water using a
watering can with a rose attached.

**IT'S NOT JUST THE ROOTS OF
TURNIPS THAT TASTE GOOD, YOU
CAN EAT THE LEAVES, TOO!**

1

2

3

RE-SOW

RE-SOW
RADISH

Try squeezing a quick sowing of radish into section five. As soon as your spring-sown lettuces are removed, rake the soil level and make two drills 1cm (½in) deep and 15cm (6in) apart. Sow seeds thinly along them, cover with soil, and water well. Radish can be ready to harvest in just four weeks, so sowings made now will be ready to pick during August (*see pp44–45*). If the roots fail to develop due to a lack of sunlight, harvest the leaves as you would a microgreen (*see p175*).

FILL-IN CROP
Radishes are ideal for filling soil that would otherwise remain bare between crops.

PEAS

**TRANSPLANT
TO HARVEST**
7–11 weeks

LIGHT
Full sun

**PLANTING
DISTANCE**
10cm (4in) apart

HARDINESS
Fully hardy

KEY PESTS
Birds
Pea moth
Powdery mildew

HARVEST
September

Once your peas are 7–10cm (2¾–4in) tall they will be ready for transplanting. If you have grown a dwarf variety, such as 'Meteor', then find a few twiggy sticks, about 50cm (20in) long, to push into the soil and act as supports for the tendrils of the peas to latch on to as they climb upwards. If you are growing a taller variety, check the final height and use larger pea sticks as required.

TRANSPLANT INTO THE BED

Once your peas have been hardened off they are quick and simple to plant out in a single row. They have strong roots and are easy to pull out of their containers by their tough stems, which makes them unlikely to be damaged during transplanting. Transplant your peas as early in July as possible, to give your plants more time to develop pods.

PRUNINGS FROM CONIFERS MAKE EXCELLENT SUPPORTS FOR PEA PLANTS TO LATCH ON TO, BUT ANY STRONG, BRANCHED CUTTINGS WILL WORK WELL.

1. Water the seedlings before transplanting. Gently pull one seedling out of its container.

2. Use your hand or a trowel to make a hole slightly larger than the root system of the plant, around 5cm (2in) from the long side of the raised bed. Place the seedling in the hole, so that the top of its root ball is level with the soil surface, and firmly press the compost around it with your fingers.

3. Repeat the same process with the remaining seedlings roughly every 7–10cm (2¾–4in) along the width of the raised bed. Water your row of pea seedlings thoroughly from a watering can fitted with a rose.

4. Push branched supporting sticks firmly into the soil between the pea seedlings and the edge of the bed. Within a few days of transplanting, the peas will begin latching on to the sticks with their thin tendrils. Encourage them in the right direction, so they don't latch on to the neighbouring beans.

ALL YOU NEED TO SUPPORT DWARF PEA
VARIETIES ARE SOME BRANCHED TWIGS.
THE TENDRILS OF THE PEAS LATCH ON
TO THE TWIGS, ALLOWING THE PLANTS TO
CLIMB UPWARDS. I USE BRANCHES FROM
OLD CHRISTMAS TREES FOR MY PEA STICKS.

GROW ON
KALE

**TRANSPLANT
TO HARVEST**
14–18 weeks

LIGHT
Full sun or
partial shade

**PLANTING
DISTANCE**
30cm (1ft) apart

HARDINESS
Fully hardy

KEY PESTS
Birds
Cabbage root fly
Caterpillars

HARVEST
November to April

Your kale will fill the space taken by your broad beans in sections three and four. Once harvested, cut the broad bean stems at the base, leaving the nitrogen-rich roots in the soil to fuel the kale's leafy, green growth. It's also best not to dig over the soil, because a firm soil keeps kale's tall stems anchored in windy weather. If the soil in your bed is loose, walk on sections three and four after planting, gently firming the soil around each seedling with your feet.

TRANSPLANT INTO THE BED
Kale grows to an impressive size and needs to be given plenty of space to reach its full potential, so don't be tempted to squeeze extra plants in. Once your plants are hardened off, transplanting them is a quick and simple process.

1. Mark out four planting positions about 30cm (1ft) apart down the middle of section three. Then repeat for section four. Take a plant, place one hand over the top of the pot to catch the seedling, and turn the pot upside down. Tap the pot with your other hand to gently free the roots.

2. Use your hands or a trowel to create a hole at one of your marked planting positions. Ensure the hole is deeper than your kale seedling's root ball. You may want to give the plant a nutrient boost by adding a handful of fresh compost to the hole at this stage, but remember to make the hole a little deeper so that the plant's root ball still fits below the surface of the soil.

3. Place the root ball of the seedling into the hole, so its top is just below the soil surface, and firmly push the soil in around it. Repeat the process for the rest of your seedlings, and soak each one thoroughly after planting, using a watering can with a rose attached.

1

2

3

GROW ON

BROAD BEANS

Water these large plants thoroughly every four to five days in hot, dry weather to keep the last of their pods swelling.

GROW ON

SWISS CHARD

Watch out for pest damage to the large leaves of Swiss chard. This can be caused by leaf mining insects, slugs, snails, and birds, such as sparrows. Water during dry spells to keep the plants in good condition.

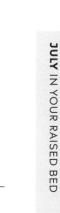

GROW ON

LEEKS

Keep your leeks watered regularly during hot summer weather to help them grow as large as possible for winter harvests. This will also help to prevent them from bolting.

GROW ON

TURNIPS AND BEETROOT

Your turnip (*top right*) and beetroot (*top left*) sowings will now have transformed into a thick row of seedlings competing with each other for space, and so will need to be thinned out.

It is important to thin out these seedlings while they are small, to give them the area they need to develop good roots. Move along the rows of seedlings, cutting the stems of the weaker seedlings with scissors to prevent disturbance to the roots of

the remaining seedlings. The tops of the thinned plants can be added to salads, or dropped onto your compost pile.

Thin the rows several times as the seedlings grow, to eventually leave both the turnip and beetroot plants about 5cm (2in) apart.

Turnip seedlings often have small holes in the leaves caused by flea beetles. These are nothing to worry about, as they won't affect how well the seedlings develop.

GROW ON

RUNNER BEANS

Pinch out, or cut off, the growing tips of the plants when they reach the top of their wigwams (*see "Grow on Broad beans", p93*). This is known as "stopping the

plants", and helps to concentrate their energy on flower and bean production (*opposite*). Don't be tempted to eat these tops – just add them to your compost pile.

GROW ON

DWARF FRENCH BEANS

Densely planted, these compact beans usually keep each other upright, but if any fall over under the weight of developing beans add extra support by pushing a twig into the soil to prop them up.

HARVEST
SWISS CHARD

I love the ease of harvesting chard! Within a matter of seconds, you have a handful of stems and leaves ready for cooking. Its delicious, slightly earthy flavour makes chard lovely steamed, stir-fried, or added to soups and stews.

HOW TO HARVEST
Now that the plants are sturdy, with large leaves, use your hands to snap off up to half of the largest stalks from a plant at each picking (*see opposite*). You can also use a knife to cut the stems at about 5cm (2in) above soil level. Harvesting the outer leaves encourages chard to send up new shoots from the middle of the plant, so return later in the month for more pickings.

Pick leaves as you need them or, like me, harvest them in big batches to blanch and freeze, and eat them throughout the year.

HARVEST
BROAD BEANS

Broad beans will be plentiful in July. Fresh baby broad beans taste lovely eaten straight from the pod, but also make a great addition to early summer risottos and pasta dishes. The pods can also be eaten whole until they are finger thick. Beans freeze well if popped from the pods, blanched, and then put into freezer bags – squeeze as much air as possible out of the bag. Eat the beans within six months of freezing.

HOW TO HARVEST
Twist or cut at the base of the pod to harvest when the outline of the beans is visible through the pod. Pop the pale green beans from their fluffy beds and enjoy. Once fully harvested, cut the stems to the ground and compost the tops, leaving the nitrogen-rich roots in the soil.

AUGUST

BEST THING ABOUT AUGUST
You can enjoy snacking on the first
peas you pop from their pods

WORST THING ABOUT AUGUST
Noticeably shorter days
signal the end of summer

WATCH OUT FOR IN AUGUST
Hot, dry weather means plants need
watering – even if you are away on holiday

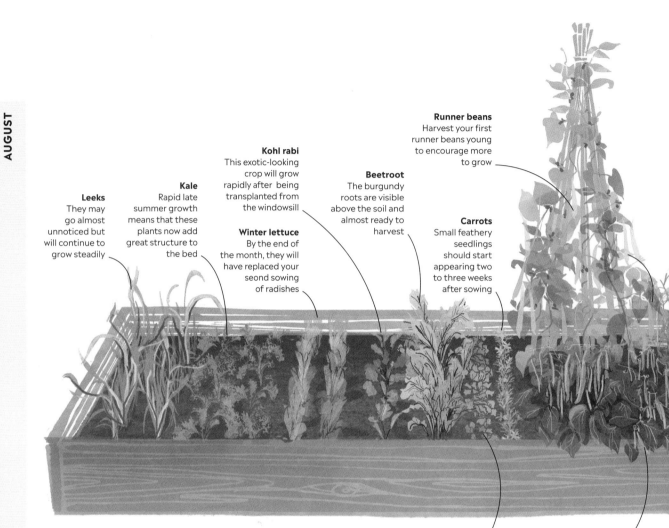

Leeks
They may go almost unnoticed but will continue to grow steadily

Kale
Rapid late summer growth means that these plants now add great structure to the bed

Kohl rabi
This exotic-looking crop will grow rapidly after being transplanted from the windowsill

Winter lettuce
By the end of the month, they will have replaced your seond sowing of radishes

Beetroot
The burgundy roots are visible above the soil and almost ready to harvest

Runner beans
Harvest your first runner beans young to encourage more to grow

Carrots
Small feathery seedlings should start appearing two to three weeks after sowing

Turnips
The leafy tops will be growing quickly, with the fat roots developing underneath

Dwarf French beans
Pluck pods by snapping their stems between your thumb and forefinger

AUGUST
AT A GLANCE

August is the bridge between summer and autumn, when there is still so much growing and plenty to harvest. Carrots take the last space to fill your bed, which is already packed with maturing crops sown in spring and early summer. Picking the first fresh peas and beans is always a highlight for me.

HOW THE BED WILL LOOK
Your bed will be packed with ten different crops as August draws to a close, and will be at the peak of its productivity. Mature beans and peas dominate one end of the bed, while lettuce, leeks, kale, and root crops continue to grow strongly.

ON THE PLAN

Carrots and kohl rabi join the bed to fill bare soil left after harvesting summer crops, while winter lettuces replace your second sowing of radishes. Established crops continue to grow.

KEY

- Start off
- Transplant
- Grow on
- Harvest
- 1 Section number

Leeks
2 rows

Winter lettuce
2 rows

Beetroot
1 row

Runner beans
8 plants

1 2 3 4 5 6 7 8 9 10

Kale
2 rows

Kohl rabi
1 row

Turnips
1 row

Carrots
1 row

Dwarf French beans
3 rows

Peas
1 row

Peas
Start snacking on sugary peas as soon as the smooth pods swell

---

ON THE WINDOWSILL

Start off

- Sow fast-growing kohl rabi on the windowsill to transplant later this month.
- Sow more Swiss chard into individual modules for a colourful autumn crop.

Grow on

- Water winter lettuces to keep them healthy before planting out this month.

IN THE RAISED BED

Start off

- Sow carrot seeds directly into a shallow drill in section eight's empty soil.

Grow on

- Remove your first crop of Swiss chard, and transplant kohl rabi into its place.
- Transplant winter lettuces into section five and water them in well.
- Check the leaves of your kale plants for caterpillars (and holes in the leaves).
- Water your radishes during dry weather to help them mature quickly, and your peas and runner beans to help their pods swell.
- Ensure that your leeks continue to grow by keeping them well watered.
- Water your rows of beetroot and turnips to keep their roots growing and prevent them from becoming tough.

HARVEST

- Enjoy peas at their sweetest – eaten in the garden, straight from the pod.
- Pick the first tender runner bean pods when they reach about 20cm (8in) long.
- Harvest dwarf French beans regularly to catch them while they are young, tender, and stringless.
- Pick the last of your first crop of Swiss chard leaves and radishes.

MAINTENANCE CHECKLIST

- Water.
- Weed.
- Watch out for pests.
- Remove spent crops.
- Harden off plants, even in warm weather.

121

ON YOUR

WINDOWSILL

Sowing vegetables on the windowsill during August gives you the opportunity to fast-track crops for a quick autumn harvest. Sow Swiss chard and kohl rabi alongside your young winter plants.

START OFF

KOHL RABI

SEED TO TRANSPLANT
4 weeks

POSITION
Warm, sunny windowsill

WATER
Every 2–3 days

TRANSPLANT
End of August

HARVEST
November

HUW'S TOP VARIETIES
'Azure Star'
'Gigante'
'White Delicacy'

With its strange globe-shaped, swollen stem sprouting long-stemmed leaves, this may be the coolest vegetable you grow in your raised bed this year! Kohl rabi is a member of the cabbage family, like your radishes and kale, and comes in attractive pale green or purple varieties, which really stand out in the garden. It is both easy and quick to grow, and is ready to harvest when the swollen stems are about the size of a ping-pong ball. They have a delicious mild, sweet, turnip-like flavour.

SOWING KOHL RABI

Sow the seeds into a tray of modules right at the very beginning of August. Kohl rabi has an excellent germination rate, so one seed per module will be enough. The seedlings will be ready to transplant in about four weeks, which will be perfectly timed to fill the space left when the first crop of Swiss chard is removed from the raised bed.

POSITION KOHL RABI SEEDLINGS ON A WINDOWSILL THAT RECEIVES AT LEAST SIX HOURS OF SUNLIGHT EACH DAY TO ALLOW THEM TO GROW STRONGLY.

1. Fill the modules with multi-purpose compost, checking that each module is properly filled by pressing the compost down firmly.

2. Make a 1cm (½in) deep hole in the centre of each module using a pencil.

3. Carefully pop one small seed into each hole, cover over with compost, and water thoroughly. Place the seed tray on a sunny windowsill and water every two or three days, when the surface of the compost is dry.

START OFF
SWISS CHARD

SEED TO TRANSPLANT
4 weeks

POSITION
A warm windowsill in full sun or part shade

WATER
Every 2–3 days

TRANSPLANT
September

HARVEST
October and November

HUW'S TOP VARIETIES
'Bright Lights'
'Magenta Sunset'
'Rhubarb Chard'

Early August is the time to get a second batch of Swiss chard under way. It is such a productive vegetable that even though the warmth of summer is almost over, you can sow it this month to transplant once the runner and dwarf French beans have been taken out in September, and still expect many leaves to harvest in autumn. The leaves won't be as big as those you picked during summer, but they will taste just as good. You can also sow Swiss chard directly into the raised bed until mid-September, in mild areas, to provide a harvest of baby leaves.

SOWING SWISS CHARD

The easiest way to sow Swiss chard for transplanting is into trays of individual modules. This late crop won't grow to reach its full size, which means you can plant them closer together. Sow 30–40 seeds to provide plenty of plants for the space. On a warm windowsill the seeds will germinate in about five days.

1

2

1. Fill the tray with multi-purpose compost. Press the compost down firmly in each module to ensure they are all properly filled, and then use your finger to make a 1cm (½in) deep hole in the centre of each.

2. Drop two seeds into each hole, cover with compost, and give the modules a thorough watering. Place the seed tray on your windowsill and water the seedlings every two to three days, when the top 1cm (½in) of the compost in each module is dry.

SWISS CHARD "SEEDS" ARE ACTUALLY A CLUSTER OF SEEDS, SO DON'T BE SURPRISED IF MORE THAN ONE PLANT GROWS IN EACH MODULE. JUST CUT THE STEMS OFF THE SMALLEST SEEDLINGS WITH SCISSORS, LEAVING THE LARGEST ONES TO GROW STRONGLY.

GROW ON
LETTUCE

GROWING ON UP
Water your lettuce seedlings lightly every day to ensure they don't dry out.

By mid-August, each module will be filled with a sturdy young plant, almost ready for transplanting. To acclimatize them to outdoor conditions, harden them off over about ten days (*see p13*). Water daily because the roots of each plant should now almost fill its module and will quickly dry the compost out. If the plants begin wilting on a sunny windowsill, move them to a shadier position that is out of full sun in the afternoon.

IN YOUR

RAISED BED

Hardly any bare soil will be visible as summer crops become ready to harvest and those planted for autumn and winter continue to mature. Any gaps will quickly be filled with seedlings from your windowsill.

START OFF
CARROTS

SEED TO HARVEST
10 weeks for "early" varieties

LIGHT
Full sun

PLANTING DISTANCE
1cm (½in)

HARDINESS
Moderately hardy

KEY PROBLEMS
Aphids
Carrot fly

HARVEST
October

HUW'S TOP VARIETIES
'Amsterdam Forcing'
'Ideal'
'Early Nantes'

Carrots are a fabulous vegetable to grow, and it's a joy to be met with the wonderful smell of fresh carrots as you pull out the brightly coloured roots in autumn. Choose fast-maturing "early" varieties for August sowings, because "maincrop" varieties will not be ready before winter. Carrots are not as easy to grow as other root vegetables, thanks to a common insect pest called carrot fly, but there are many ways to work around this problem and reduce the risk of failure (*see box opposite*).

SOWING DIRECTLY INTO THE BED
Sow carrots thinly during the first week of August, at a shallow depth of around ½cm (¼in). Germination can take up to three weeks, but watering every day or two during dry weather will keep the soil consistently moist and help the seeds to grow as quickly as possible.

1

2

3

COPING WITH CARROT FLY

The strong smell of carrot roots attracts these troublesome pests. They lay their eggs at the base of the leaves, where the larvae hatch and tunnel into your carrot roots. Follow these tips and put prevention measures in place to stop this happening to your crop.

1. Sow later in the season (summer, not spring) to reduce the risk of attack.

2. Sow seeds thinly to avoid having to thin the seedlings, which releases the carrot scent and attracts adult flies to lay their eggs.

3. Grow carrot varieties that show resistance to the pest, such as 'Resistafly' and 'Maestro'.

4. Don't grow carrots in the same place every year, as carrot fly pupae can overwinter in the soil and produce more flies in spring.

5. Create a barrier of insect-proof netting, at least 60cm (2ft) high, around the perimeter of the seedlings to prevent these low-flying insects from reaching them.

DAMAGED ROOTS
Carrot fly larvae burrow through roots, leaving networks of brown tunnels that allow rot to set in and spoil your crop.

1. In the middle of the empty soil in section eight, stretch a string line across the width of the bed. Draw your rake handle along it to create a trench, or simply lay a piece of bamboo cane across the bed, and push it down about ½cm (¼in). Remove the cane and you will have a perfect trench in which to sow seeds.

2. Sow the seeds thinly, dropping in one or two seeds per 1cm/½in. This avoids the need for thinning later, which can attract carrot flies to your seedlings to lay their eggs.

3. Gently cover the trench with soil and use a watering can with a fine rose to water the trench. Watering straight from the spout of the can would damage the trench and send seeds everywhere. Label the trench and water it regularly during dry weather.

127

GROW ON

KOHL RABI

**TRANSPLANT
TO HARVEST**
10 weeks

LIGHT
Full sun or light shade

**PLANTING
DISTANCE**
15cm (6in) apart

HARDINESS
Moderately hardy

KEY PROBLEMS
Birds, cabbage root
fly, slugs and snails

HARVEST
November

At the end of August, just four weeks after sowing, transplant your kohl rabi seedlings into their final growing positions in section six of your bed. Avoid planting them too close together, as a lack of space makes them prone to flowering prematurely, known as "bolting"; this causes their stems to become woody and inedible.

TRANSPLANT INTO THE BED

Allow your seedlings to get accustomed to outdoor conditions by moving them outside for a longer period each day over three days to harden them off (*see p13*). When the seedlings are ready to plant,

mark a row across the width of the bed, about 20cm (8in) away from the beetroot, using a bamboo cane or a string line.

AFTER REMOVING THE SPENT SWISS CHARD WITH A FORK, MAKE SURE YOU RAKE THE SOIL FLAT TO PREPARE IT FOR THE KOHL RABI BEING TRANSPLANTED.

1

2

1. Remove the stumps of the harvested Swiss chard, add some fresh compost to the soil to provide your kohl rabi with extra nutrients, and give the soil a quick rake to even it out. Using your hand, make the first planting hole 10cm (4in) from the long side of the raised bed. It should be slightly wider and deeper than the seedling's roots. Gently push the roots from the module and hold it by a leaf.

2. Place the seedling into the hole so that the soil is level with the top of the root ball. Firm the soil around it with your fingers.

3. Plant a seedling in the same way every 15cm (6in) along the row. You should fit eight plants along the row. Once you have finished planting, water each seedling throughly to wet the soil around its roots.

3

GOING ON HOLIDAY
Heading away on a summer holiday can be a stressful time for gardeners! If you're going away and there isn't any rain forecast or you have lots of seedlings growing on the windowsill, what's the best thing to do?

Away for three to five days
The morning that you leave, soak the soil in the raised bed with five or six full watering cans. This will be more than enough to see your plants through. Give your seedlings on the windowsill a good soak and place cardboard against the window to shield the compost from sunlight. This will reduce evaporation and keep the compost moist.

Away for more than five days
If you plan a longer trip then seek the help of a friend or neighbour. Move any seedlings on your windowsill to their home and show them how to water them every two or three days. Ask someone to water your raised bed every three or four days (or less often if there is heavy rain) using four to six full watering cans. Thank your helper with a share of your home-grown produce.

GROW ON

WINTER LETTUCE

TRANSPLANT TO HARVEST
4–6 weeks

LIGHT
Full sun or partial shade

PLANTING DISTANCE
5–8cm (2–3in)

HARDINESS
Moderately hardy

KEY PROBLEMS
Aphids
Slugs and snails

HARVEST
September to October

From mid-August, once you have finished your second sowing of radish, your lettuce seedlings will be ready to transplant into section five (between the kohl rabi and the kale). If the large kale plants are looming over this space and shading the row, pick and eat a few of the biggest kale leaves to make room for the lettuce.

TRANSPLANT INTO THE BED

Even in late summer, make sure that your seedlings have been "hardened off" by acclimatizing them to outdoor conditions gradually for a few days (*see p13*). Beware of hungry slugs and snails during this time, because they will just as happily feed on seedlings growing in containers as on those planted in the raised bed.

THERE'S NO NEED TO WASTE YOUR SPARE WINTER LETTUCE SEEDLINGS. CUT OFF THE LEAVES AND ADD THEM TO A SALAD.

1

2

3

1. Push the roots of the seedling up from the base of the module and hold it by the top of its root ball rather than by the leaves. Make a planting hole 10cm (4in) from the long edge of the bed using your hand. Ensure that the hole is slightly deeper and wider than the roots.

2. Place the the seedling into the hole, so that the top of its root ball is level with the soil. Push soil around the roots with your fingers.

3. Firm the roots of the seedling into the soil with your hand. Plant a seedling every 5–8cm (2–3in) along the row and water each plant thoroughly.

GROW ON

KALE

Check the leaves for pests, because the foliage of curly and blistered varieties makes the perfect place for caterpillars, aphids, and cabbage whitefly to hide. Regularly picking off any pests that you find should keep them under control.

GROW ON

RADISHES

Keep these spicy roots well watered to fuel their growth and help to prevent them flowering prematurely or "bolting", which makes the roots tough.

GROW ON

LEEKS

Because your leeks haven't required much attention, some weeds may have popped up around them that you hadn't spotted. Make sure to check regularly and pull them out while they are small.

A few orange spots may develop on the leaves of your leeks. This is leek rust, a fungal disease that often occurs in hot, dry weather. Although it looks unsightly, the plants will continue to grow untroubled.

KEEP YOUR BEANS AND PEAS WELL
WATERED. THEY MAY STRUGGLE
TO PRODUCE HEALTHY PODS IF
LEFT IN DRIED-OUT SOIL.

DWARF AND RUNNER BEANS

These vigorous plants don't like drying out during hot, dry weather, and will keep cropping for longer if they are watered regularly throughout August.

GROW ON

PEAS

Keep your peas well watered so that the pods develop and swell until they are ready to harvest. This is especially important in hot, dry weather.

GROW ON

BEETROOT AND TURNIPS

Ensure that these crops have moist soil by watering them regularly during dry spells. This will enable them to grow strongly, ready for harvesting next month.

HARD WORK PAYS OFF
Your row of beetroot will mature rapidly during August if given plenty of water.

**SWEETEST
LITTLE THING**
For me, there's nothing
quite the same as
eating the first peas
of the season and
remembering how
fantastic they taste
straight from the pod.

HARVEST
PEAS

I think that the best way to enjoy peas is
to eat them straight from the pod. Cooking
fresh peas gives you delicious results, but
I prefer to eat them the instant that they are
picked, as a raw, sweet and flavourful snack.

HOW TO HARVEST
Keep a close eye on your peas to catch
them while they're young and tender.
Shelling peas and sugarsnaps are ready
to pick when their pods are swollen and
rounded, but still smooth and bright green.
Mangetout varieties need to be picked
when the pod is large and flat. Simply pick
them from the plant with a firm pull of their
stem, holding on to the plant so that it
doesn't come away from its supports.
Remember that after harvesting, peas
rapidly turn their sugars into starch and
lose their sweetness, so eat them quickly.

CATCH THEM QUICK
Pods will darken and become crinkled in
texture as they mature. Harvest them
promptly if you want to eat the pods whole.

IT'S RARE TO HAVE PROBLEMS
WITH RUNNER BEANS. IN FACT,
I'VE NEVER SEEN A PLANT THAT
ISN'T DOING WELL – AND I VISIT
PLENTY OF GARDENS!

HARVEST
RUNNER BEANS

Eight of these large, climbing plants will
produce a huge crop if you keep picking
the beans to encourage more to form.
Runner beans sometimes suffer from a
lack of pods forming or "setting" after
flowering. This is most often due to hot,
dry weather, but incorrect soil pH, a lack of
pollinating insects, and insufficient organic
matter in the soil can also contribute.

HOW TO HARVEST
Pick the pods by pulling their stems
away from the plant. Runner beans
can be picked at three different stages
of maturity:

- **Young pods** are picked when they are
about 20cm (8in) long. They are bright
green, tender, and ready to cook after just
cutting off their tops and tails.
- **Larger pods** need to have the tough
edges of the pod cut off before cooking.
Bigger pods increase your harvest, but they
do become tougher. When pods begin to
roughen and darken in colour they need
to be harvested quickly.
- **Mature beans** can still be eaten once
the outside pod is too tough. Pick any
remaining pods when you take down the
wigwam in September. Pop the beans from
the pods and dry them on a windowsill,
flipping them over after a few days to dry
both sides. After two weeks, store the
beans in an airtight container in a cool
place. To cook, soak the beans for 12 hours
in cold water and boil gently until tender.

HARVEST
DWARF FRENCH BEANS

BEANS ON THE SIDE
I boil my beans for about five minutes, and then add some butter, crushed garlic, and a pinch of salt to make a delicious side dish!

These incredibly productive little plants will keep you supplied with fine, tender beans for weeks. Once you're used to enjoying them this fresh you won't want to go back to the lacklustre flavour and stringy texture of the shop-bought kind.

HOW TO HARVEST
Pick your dwarf French bean pods by cutting their stems with scissors or snapping them off with your fingers. They are ready when they are slender and 8–10cm (3–4in) long. If they grow larger they can become tough and less appetizing. Cut off the tops and tails of the beans before cooking.

CONTINUE TO HARVEST
RADISHES AND SWISS CHARD

You'll be harvesting the last of your radishes and Swiss chard leaves this month. If your radishes haven't developed roots, just harvest the leaves, eating them in salads.

You will need to remove the roots of your Swiss chard plants to make space for your kohl rabi, so once the final leaves have been removed, dig out the stumps using a fork. Shake any soil off the roots and add them to your compost pile.

When your radishes are all harvested, simply rake the soil level so that it is ready for your winter lettuce to be transplanted into it.

SEPTEMBER

BEST THING ABOUT SEPTEMBER
Cooler, sunny autumn days are perfect
for working outside in the garden

WORST THING ABOUT SEPTEMBER
Shortening days and colder weather
restrict what can be sown successfully

WATCH OUT FOR IN SEPTEMBER
"Freak" early frosts that damage or kill tender
plants are possible in cooler regions

Leeks
These well-established plants will continue to develop nicely

Kale
Strong-stemmed, with a good head of leaves, your kale is nearly mature

Winter lettuce
Although only transplanted in August, it will be ready to harvest by the end of this month

Kohl rabi
Now that it has settled in it will start developing quickly

Mustard leaves
Sow these spicy leaves to pep up autumn salads

Carrots
Keep these seedlings growing strongly by watering during dry spells

Spinach
Watch out for bright green seedlings appearing about ten days after sowing

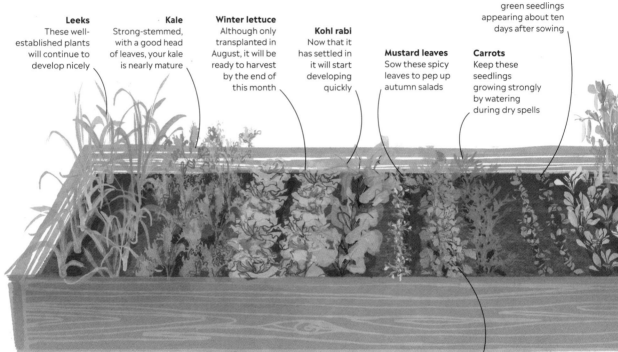

Turnips
Pull up these gorgeous white or purple-topped roots to enjoy in September stews

Swiss chard
Thanks to the head start these seedlings got on the windowsill, they will be coming along well

SEPTEMBER AT A GLANCE

As autumn creeps in, growth slows, plants look less vibrant, and it's too late to sow all but the quickest-growing salads. Your harvest basket will be filled with peas, beans, and root vegetables, though, and colder nights aren't a concern, because the crops in your bed can all cope with any light frosts.

HOW THE BED WILL LOOK

During September you will notice a real change in the raised bed as the last of the tall summer beans and peas are harvested and cleared. An attractive range of lower-growing leafy greens and root crops will replace them for autumn and winter.

ON THE PLAN
Removing the beans leaves a generous space to plant rows of young Swiss chard plants and sow spinach seeds. A row of mustard can also be sown once you have picked your beetroot.

KEY

Start off

Transplant

Grow on

Harvest

1 | Section number

Peas
Relish harvesting the last of your sweet home-grown peas

| **Leeks** 2 rows | | | **Winter lettuce** 2 rows | | **Mustard leaves** 1 row | **Carrots** 1 row | **Swiss chard** 2 rows |

Sections: 1 2 3 4 5 6 7 8 9 10

Kale 2 rows — **Kohl rabi** 1 row — **Turnips** 1 row — **Spinach** 2 rows — **Peas** 1 row

---

ON THE WINDOWSILL
Start off
• Sow tatsoi into newspaper pots and germinate on a sunny windowsill.

Grow on
• Water your Swiss chard seedlings when the top of the compost is dry, and begin to harden them off ready for transplanting.

IN THE RAISED BED
Start off
• Sow spinach and mustard leaves directly into the soil; they germinate well in the cooler September weather.

Grow on
• Grow your Swiss chard more densely than you did your spring-sown crop (see pp70–71), because you are growing smaller plants for baby leaves.
• Add stakes to support tall kale plants during windy autumn weather.
• If necessary, thin your carrot seedlings early in the month. Compost any thinnings to ensure that they don't attract carrot flies to your raised bed.
• Remove the stems and leaves of your dwarf French and runner beans from the bed, leaving their roots in the soil. Check the stems for any remaining pods before you compost them.

HARVEST
• Cut the first leaves from the outer parts of your winter lettuces.
• Pull up your beetroot and turnips by gripping the base of their leaves and giving a firm tug.
• Don't miss the last pods on your dwarf French beans, runner beans, and peas.

MAINTENANCE CHECKLIST
• Water.
• Weed.
• Turn your compost.
• Build a leaf mould bay.
• Compost waste.
• Watch out for pests.

139

ON YOUR WINDOWSILL

There will be fewer crops on your windowsill now that it is almost too late in the year to transplant them outdoors. There's still time, however, to plant out your Swiss chard and raise tatsoi seedlings for a late crop.

START OFF
TATSOI

SEED TO TRANSPLANT
4 weeks

POSITION
A cool spot in full sun or partial shade

WATER
Every 2 days

TRANSPLANT
October

HARVEST
November

A member of the brassica family, this Asian vegetable is similar to cabbage, but much more delicately flavoured and easier to grow – it is well worth trying. Tatsoi is also fast-growing, which makes it an ideal quick crop to follow any vegetables harvested in early autumn. Sowing at this time of year, when the days are cooling and shortening, also means that you don't need to worry about your plants bolting (running to seed prematurely), a common problem when growing tatsoi in hot, dry summer conditions. Once the plant bolts, the leaves become bitter and unpalatable.

SOWING TATSOI INTO NEWSPAPER POTS

Sow your seed as early in September as possible, so you can transplant before the weather gets too cold. Tatsoi seedlings hate root disturbance during transplanting, so always sow them into biodegradable pots, such as home-made newspaper pots (*see pp142–143*), which will break down as the roots grow through them into the soil.

1. Make your newspaper pots and fill them three-quarters full with multi-purpose compost.

2. Use a pencil to create a small hole, about 1cm (½in) deep, in the centre of each pot. Drop two seeds into each hole.

3. Add compost to the top of the pot to cover the seeds and fill in the hole.

4. Arrange the newspaper pots in a large container or on a tray and place it on your windowsill. Water thoroughly and keep the compost moist, but not wet. Seeds should germinate after one to two weeks. Don't worry if the newspaper pots begin to break apart – they will still hold their shape well.

CROP SWAP

You can grow Chinese cabbage, mizuna, komatsuna, or pak choi using the same instructions as given for tatsoi. Sow seed in September, transplant into your bed in October, and harvest from November.

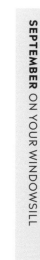

MAKE NEWSPAPER POTS

Pots made from folded and rolled newspaper are useful containers for starting seedlings. They decompose in the soil, and so are a great way to reuse waste paper. The safety of printing inks on the paper is a concern – avoid glossy paper, or any ink that smudges or leaves residue on your finger when you rub it. Making newspaper pots is a great job for a dark and dismal day when the weather stops you getting out and about in the garden. You will need a special tool for making paper pots – buy one cheaply or borrow one from a friend.

1. Mark one-and-a-half times the length of the pot maker's cylinder on your newspaper, and cut the paper into straight strips 30cm (1ft) long. The overhanging paper will form the base of the pot.

2. Take two newspaper strips (to double the paper's thickness) and roll them tightly around the cylinder together.

3. Fold the overhanging newspaper in towards the cylinder of the pot maker to form a flat base for the pot.

4. Press the cylinder wrapped with paper down hard into the base of the pot maker.

5 Twisting while pressing ensures a tightly folded base and results in a sturdier pot.

6. Remove the newspaper pot from the pot maker. Repeat this process until you have all the pots you need.

1

2

4

5

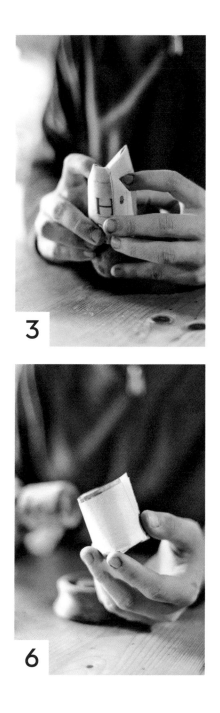

3

6

SWISS CHARD

Water your developing seedlings regularly when the top of the compost in their modules feels dry. Several seedlings are likely to have appeared in each of the modules. Thin out the weaker seedlings by snipping the base of their stems with scissors, leaving the roots of the strongest seedling undisturbed. You should be left with one healthy seedling growing strongly in each module.

IF YOU DON'T HAVE MANY SWISS CHARD SEEDLINGS, YOU CAN GET AWAY WITH NOT THINNING THEM AS THEY ARE ONLY BEING GROWN FOR BABY LEAVES.

IN YOUR RAISED BED

The bed is full and yielding delicious beetroot, turnips, and lettuce this month. As September progresses, the removal of your beans and beetroot creates space for late sowings of spinach and mustard, and for transplanting Swiss chard.

START OFF

SPINACH

SEED TO HARVEST
6–7 weeks

LIGHT
Full sun or partial shade

PLANTING DISTANCE
1cm (½in) apart

HARDINESS
Fully hardy

KEY PROBLEMS
Birds
Slugs and snails
Downy mildew

HARVEST
October and November

HUW'S TOP VARIETIES
'Amazon'
'Early Prickly Seeded'
'Matador'

Spinach is a fast-growing, hardy salad crop. It is suited to autumn sowing, because it is prone to flowering prematurely, known as "bolting", in hot summer weather, which stops plants producing new leaves for picking. Sown now, spinach will produce a bumper crop of the smaller leaves familiar from supermarket salad bags, and often labelled as baby spinach. Two rows of spinach will fit into your raised bed; put the first in half of section eight (15cm/6in from the row of carrots) and the second next to them in half of section nine (another 15cm/6in along).

SOW DIRECTLY INTO THE BED
As early in September as possible, prepare the soil where your bean crops have been removed by raking it level. If space is not available for sowing at the beginning of the month, then try raising seedlings in modules on the windowsill to plant out in three to four weeks, once the beans have been harvested and dug out.

IF YOU'RE EVER STRUGGLING FOR SPACE IN YOUR BED, ROWS OF SALAD CROPS CAN BE SOWN AND PLANTED CLOSER TOGETHER TO MAKE SPACE FOR VEGETABLES THAT NEED MORE ROOM.

1

2

3

1. Create a trench about 2.5cm (1in) deep across the width of the bed, by laying a bamboo cane on the soil and pressing it down firmly.

2. Sprinkle seed along the row using your thumb and forefinger, aiming to leave one seed every 1cm (½in) along the length of the trench.

3. Pull soil over the trench to cover the seeds lightly. Water thoroughly with a watering can fitted with a rose, to avoid large quantities of water washing away soil and seeds.

145

START OFF

MUSTARD LEAVES

SEED TO HARVEST
5–6 weeks for
salad leaves

LIGHT
Full sun

**PLANTING
DISTANCE**
4cm (1½in) apart

HARDINESS
Fully hardy

KEY PROBLEMS
Slugs and snails

HARVEST
October

**HUW'S TOP
VARIETIES**
'Red Frills'
'Red Giant'

To add something new and a little exciting to the bed, try this unusual, fast-growing salad crop. Mustard 'Red Frills' is a variety of Asian leaf mustard with attractive, purple, serrated leaves and a peppery taste that intensifies as the leaves mature. There are many varieties of mustard to try, along with other interesting salad leaves, such as mizuna and rocket. Seed mixes are also available, which allow you to grow several types of salad in a single row.

SOW DIRECTLY INTO THE BED

Mustard leaves are an ideal quick crop to sow following your beetroot. After harvesting the beetroot from section seven, lightly rake the soil to remove any lumps and level it. A row of mustard seeds can then be sown straight into the ground.

1. Press a bamboo cane into the soil to create a straight trench about 1cm (½in) deep across the width of the bed.

2. Sprinkle the seeds thinly along the trench, using your thumb and forefinger. Aim to sow thinly, placing a seed every 1cm (½in). Precision isn't vital, however, because the seedlings can easily be thinned out after they emerge.

3. Cover the trench lightly with soil. Water with a watering can fitted with a rose to spread the flow of water and prevent any seeds from being washed away.

TRY SOWING DIFFERENT VARIETIES OF ASIAN SALAD LEAVES IN SEED TRAYS ON YOUR WINDOWSILL AT ANY TIME OF YEAR TO HARVEST AS MICROGREENS AFTER JUST THREE WEEKS.

CROP SWAP

You can grow rocket or mizuna using the same instructions as given for mustard leaves. Sow seed in September for a November harvest.

1

2

GROW ON

SWISS CHARD

**TRANSPLANT
TO HARVEST**
4–12 weeks

LIGHT
Full sun

**PLANTING
DISTANCE**
5–10cm (2–4in) apart

HARDINESS
Fully hardy

KEY PROBLEMS
Birds
Slugs and snails
Downy mildew

HARVEST
October and
November

Once your Swiss chard seedlings are around 5cm (2in) tall, they are ready to be gradually acclimatized to cooler outdoor conditions, or "hardened off", over the course of about five days (*see p13*). Once this has been done, they can be transplanted into the bed. It won't take long for them to grow to a size at which they can be harvested as baby leaves.

TRANSPLANT INTO THE BED

Swiss chard plants grown this late in the season will not grow to their full size, so you can squeeze plenty of plants into the space available. Aim to transplant two rows of ten plants, with one row in the empty half of section ten (15cm/6in from the peas), and the other row in the empty half of section nine (15cm/6in on from that).

1. Use a bamboo cane or string line to mark out a straight row across the width of the bed. Use your hands to make ten small holes at 10cm (4in) intervals along the row, starting 15cm (6in) from the long side of the bed.

2. Push the plants from their modules by pushing from the base with your fingers. Hold them carefully around the root ball, never by their stems. Place the seedlings in the holes, so that the tops of their root balls are level with the soil surface.

3. Bring the soil around the roots with your hands and press down to firm the plants into the ground. Water the two rows thoroughly at the roots, using a watering can fitted with a rose.

3

IF YOU DON'T WANT TO RAISE
SWISS CHARD IN MODULES,
SOW SEEDS DIRECTLY INTO THE
BED IN EARLY SEPTEMBER, USING
EXACTLY THE SAME METHOD AS
YOU DID FOR SPINACH.

GROW ON

KALE

DON'T TIE TIGHTLY
Leave a small gap when tying the stem to the cane, to allow for growth.

Tall kale plants can easily be blown over in autumn storms. Prevent this from happening by supporting them with thick bamboo canes. Push a 60cm (2ft) long cane deep into the soil close to each kale stem. Secure each stem to its cane by tying it with a short length of string.

GROW ON
LEEKS

After almost three months in the raised bed your leeks should be reaching a good size and will now make an attractive sight, standing tall in their row. They will continue to grow if watered thoroughly during any dry spells of weather, but won't be ready to harvest until winter.

GROW ON
DWARF FRENCH BEANS AND RUNNER BEANS

Your beans must now make way for spinach and Swiss chard. Remove only the leaves and stems, as the roots of bean plants contain nitrogen that benefits other plants if left in the soil. Cut the stems at soil level, and remember to check the foliage for any last pods before adding to the compost pile. If you find any runner bean pods, pop out the beans (*see right*), as they can be dried and stored for cooking (*see p134*).

BEANS IN A POD
Mature beans in runner bean pods can be popped out of their pods, then dried and stored for cooking.

GROW ON

CARROTS

There should be 2.5–4cm (1–1½in) between each of your carrot seedlings. If they are growing more densely than that, thin the seedlings by cutting off the tops with scissors. This avoids disturbing the roots of remaining plants and keeps the scent released to a minimum, helping to prevent problems with carrot fly (*see p127*).

THIN YOUR CARROTS
Your carrots should be thinned out so that they are 2.5–4cm (1-1½in) apart.

GROW ON

BEETROOT AND TURNIPS

Keep both of these root crops well watered during any periods of dry September weather. If they don't get enough water, their roots can become tough before they are big enough to harvest.

GROW ON

PEAS

Although you will have harvested most of your peas at this stage, it's important to keep the plants watered so that the final few pods grow to maturity.

GARDENER'S SNACK

I think peas are the best snack for a gardener. They're sweet, delicious, and very moreish (and also super healthy!)

GROW ON

WINTER LETTUCE

Remove any slugs and snails around these plants during wet weather to keep the outer leaves in peak condition as they become ready to harvest.

GROW ON

KOHL RABI

I love to watch these strange vegetables grow and swell rapidly in the bed. They should be trouble-free, and watering during dry weather will help to support their fast growth.

WINTER LETTUCE

Your winter lettuce will be ready to provide their first pickings of fresh, crisp salad leaves. Remove the row of lettuces next to the kale at the end of the month to make way for your tatsoi seedlings. You can continue to harvest leaves from the second row of lettuce plants until they finish cropping. Then remove the roots of the plants from the soil.

HOW TO HARVEST

Extend your harvest by just plucking the leaves you need from the outside of the plant, rather than cutting the whole head of lettuce at once. This will allow the younger leaves to keep growing and provide you with salad through autumn.

HARVEST AS NEEDED
Pull the outer leaves off your lettuce as you need them, so that the central leaves continue to grow.

HARVEST
BEETROOT

These intensely coloured root vegetables have a particularly sweet, earthy flavour when home-grown, and a silky smooth texture that is rarely found in bought beetroot. My favourite ways to eat them are roasted with olive oil, garlic, and salt, or simply steamed and tossed in butter.

HOW TO HARVEST
Beetroot will stand well in the soil until the first frosts that reach -4°C (25°F), but because you want to use its space to plant another crop, harvest the whole row in the first half of September, or the first week if you live in a cool area. Pull up the roots by gripping the base of their stems and giving them a firm tug upwards (*see below*). Knock off any excess soil and chop or twist off the leaves, which make a beautiful addition to salads. The roots are best enjoyed as fresh as possible, but will store well for a month or two in a cool, dry place. Don't keep them in a fridge, because they will quickly shrivel and dry out.

PICKING FAVOURITES
Depending on my mood, beetroot quite often finds itself at the top of my favourite vegetables to grow and eat. It's an ongoing battle between beetroot, peas, and Swiss chard.

HARVEST

TURNIPS

Keep an eye on these fast-growing roots and catch them before they get too big. When they are the size of a golf ball, they are tender enough to grate raw into salads or pop whole into stews. Once they grow larger (*see right*), they toughen, their flavour intensifies, and they should be cooked before being eaten.

HOW TO HARVEST

Check the size of your turnip roots by looking at the top of the roots poking above the soil. If roots are covered, use your fingers to push away the soil to get a better idea of their size. When they reach the size you want them, hold the base of the stems and pull upwards to unearth the root. Turnips are best kept in the soil until needed, and will survive any frosts.

FRESH IS BEST
Many people hate turnips, but I feel they just haven't experienced the joy of eating a young fresh root.

CONTINUE TO HARVEST

PEAS

Once your peas are finished, cut the stems at the soil, and leave the roots in the bed as you did your beans (*see p150*). Remember to look for any remaining pods in the foliage before you compost the stems of the plants.

OCTOBER

BEST THING ABOUT OCTOBER
The autumnal colours

WORST THING ABOUT OCTOBER
Summer is just a distant memory

WATCH OUT FOR IN OCTOBER
Places to collect fallen leaves

Leeks
They may have fattened up, but leave these plants because they have not finished growing

Kale
Harvest your first kale this month, after a long wait!

Tatsoi
Transplant into the raised bed for a November crop of crisp leaves

Kohl rabi
Watch this peculiar crop develop at a surprising speed

Mustard leaves
Cut the first of these colourful leaves towards the end of the month

Spinach
Pick baby spinach leaves as required for salads

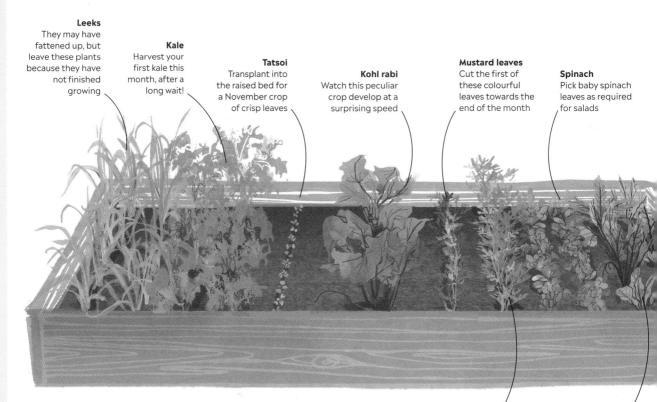

Carrots
Keep your row of carrots free of weeds, and the roots will be ready next month

Swiss chard
Start harvesting the leaves of your Swiss chard while they are young and tender

OCTOBER AT A GLANCE

Many plants start dying back or losing their leaves this month. The speed of this change always amazes me, but on the positive side, there will still be a few crops to plant, and many to harvest. You can also make good use of the fallen leaves to produce your own leaf mould.

HOW THE BED WILL LOOK
It is now that the bed takes on its autumn colours. Once the peas are lifted, all trace of summer is gone, and the tough leeks and kale suddenly stand tall. The foliage filling the rest of the bed makes a bold display.

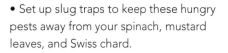

Leeks 2 rows | **Tatsoi** 1 row | **Kohl rabi** 1 row | **Empty** | **Spinach** 2 rows | **Garlic** 1 row

Sections: 1 2 3 4 5 6 7 8 9 10

Kale 2 rows | **Empty** | **Mustard leaves** 1 row | **Carrots** 1 row | **Swiss chard** 2 rows

ON THE PLAN

Garlic and tatsoi enter the bed this month, keeping it almost full. Space is made for the garlic by taking out the peas, but all of the other crops remain.

KEY

- Empty
- Start off
- Transplant
- Grow on
- Harvest
- 1 Section number

Garlic
Plant garlic cloves for an aromatic crop next summer

ON THE WINDOWSILL

Start off

- There are no new seedlings to start in October, because it will be too cold to plant them out in winter.

Grow on

- Keep watering your tatsoi seedlings while you move them outdoors for longer each day to harden them off.

IN THE RAISED BED

Start off

- Plant garlic cloves now. They will tough out the winter and eventually will be ready to harvest in midsummer.

Grow on

- Transplant your tatsoi seedlings during the first week of October, and protect them from slugs and snails.
- Weed your leeks to reduce competition for water and nutrients in the soil.
- Check that your kale and its supports are standing firm after any high winds.

- Set up slug traps to keep these hungry pests away from your spinach, mustard leaves, and Swiss chard.

Harvest

- Harvest the outer leaves of your mustard leaves and spinach to keep a succession of new leaves coming.
- Pick the first of your kale by snapping off the leaves where they join the main stem.
- Harvest baby Swiss chard leaves to add to colourful salads.

MAINTENANCE CHECKLIST

- Water.
- Weed.
- Keep watch for pests.
- Compost garden waste.
- Rake up fallen leaves to make leaf mould.

RAISED BED

Even this late in the season, garlic and tatsoi can still be planted. Salad crops and kale keep the bed full, along with the leeks, carrots, and kohl rabi that are all nearing maturity.

START OFF
GARLIC

PLANT TO HARVEST
32–38 weeks

LIGHT
Full sun

PLANTING DISTANCE
10cm (4in) apart

HARDINESS
Fully hardy

HARVEST
End of June to July

KEY PROBLEMS
Birds
Rust

HUW'S TOP VARIETIES
'Provence Wight'
'Red Duke'
'Vallelado Wight'

Garlic is a versatile vegetable for the kitchen and is also easy to grow. It spends a long time in the ground, but it is certainly worth the wait – I see it as a crop that links the end of one growing season to the start of the next. Choose named varieties for their characteristic colours, flavours, and hardiness. Alternatively, try planting organic garlic from the supermarket, which won't have been treated to prevent the cloves sprouting. Garlic is hardy enough to establish through winter, allowing it to race away in spring and mature quickly for a summer harvest, before diseases such as rust (*see pp218–219*) cause problems.

PLANT DIRECTLY INTO THE BED
Now is the perfect time to plant garlic, although it can be done any time up until Christmas. Gently split your whole bulbs of garlic into individual cloves. Check that each clove is firm and healthy, with no sunken or brown patches, and choose the largest 12 cloves for planting out.

1. Lay a tape measure across the empty half of section ten, and make a hole 5cm (2in) deep every 10cm (4in) along the tape using a bamboo cane or a dibber.

2. The top of your garlic clove is pointed and the bottom is flat. Take care to drop each clove into its hole the right way up, with the pointed end facing upwards.

3. Push soil back into each hole to fill it. Autumn rain will provide the moisture that the cloves need, so just keep the row weed-free and green shoots should appear above the soil by late winter.

PLANT THE RIGHT WAY UP
Ensure that the flat end of each clove, where roots will form, drops to the bottom of the hole.

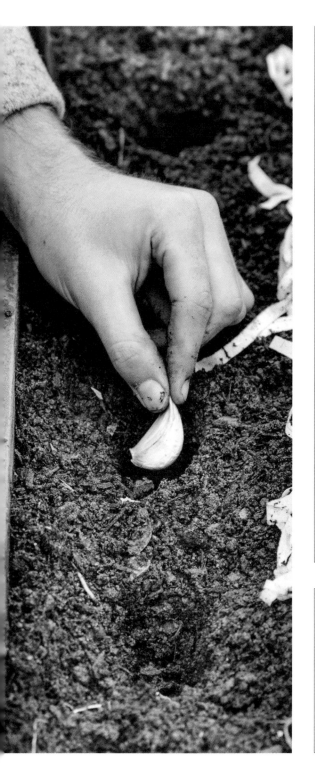

WHEN TO HARVEST GARLIC

Next summer, your garlic will be ready to harvest from the end of June onwards, when the bottom five or six leaves have turned yellow. Lift the bulbs carefully using a hand fork rather than simply pulling them up. This helps to prevent damage to the stem, which is needed intact when the bulbs are dried for storage.

Store garlic

To store your garlic, gently brush off excess soil and keep the stem and all the leaves attached to the bulb. Tie the long stems together to make bunches of five or six bulbs and hang them up in a cool, dark, dry place. Leaving them like this for a month dries out the stems and the papery wrapping around the bulbs, but retains the moisture in the cloves. Each bulb can be cut down as required for use in the kitchen.

PERFECT FOR THE KITCHEN
Once your garlic bulbs have been dried, they will keep for months, ready to add to food. Remember to save a few to plant out next year.

WHAT'S HAPPENING ON THE WINDOWSILL?

Once your tatsoi seedlings have been transplanted, your windowsill will be empty this month. That's because there is no need to start any new seedlings for the raised bed this close to winter. From November, however, this indoor growing space will be used to grow delicious crops of microgreens right through the winter.

GROW ON

TATSOI

**TRANSPLANT
TO HARVEST**
4–5 weeks

LIGHT
Full sun

**PLANTING
DISTANCE**
10cm (4in) apart

HARDINESS
Moderately hardy

KEY PROBLEMS
Cabbage root fly
Caterpillars
Flea beetle
Slugs and snails

HARVEST
November

Aim to transplant your tatsoi during the first week of October, after hardening the seedlings off by putting them outside for a little longer each day over ten days (*see p13*). Planting them early in the month will maximize the time that they have to establish and grow now that it is nearing the end of the growing season. Planted close together, the seedlings will give you a quick crop of baby leaves in November.

TRANSPLANT INTO THE BED

Once your tatsoi plants are over 5cm (2in) tall they are ready to transplant. Add a handful of multi-purpose compost to the base of the hole when planting out; this supplies extra nutrients that will keep the seedlings growing strongly. The compost you that used when you first filled your raised bed has been enough to meet the plants' needs so far, but its nutrients will now have been depleted.

1

2

SEEDLINGS ARE VULNERABLE TO SLUG DAMAGE.
AFTER TRANSPLANTING, HUNT FOR SLUGS
AT NIGHT USING A TORCH, AND REMOVE ANY
YOU FIND. SET SLUG BAIT TRAPS, TOO.

3

4

1. Mark out a line across the bed in section five with a cane or string. Use your hand to create a hole twice as deep and slightly wider than the newspaper pots, about 10cm (4in) from one long edge of the bed.

2. Half fill the hole with compost, leaving enough space for your seedling to be planted on top.

3. Put the plant – newspaper pot and all – into the hole. Push soil around the pot and press down firmly to secure it in place.

4. Repeat this for each pot, leaving about 10cm (4in) between plants. Complete the job by giving each seedling a thorough watering for a few seconds.

MAKE YOUR OWN LEAF MOULD

Start a leaf mould pile to produce a rich soil improver. Rake up leaves in your garden or get permission to collect them elsewhere, maybe a park.

Where to put your pile

Keep your leaf mould pile in a covered bin to protect it from rain. It should be separate from your main compost bin, as leaves decompose more slowly than other compost materials. If you built your own compost bin (*see pp28–29*), add an extra bay using three more pallets lined with chicken wire. Cover the top with plywood.

Which leaves to use

You can use any leaves, but those from different species will decompose at different rates. Small leaves from oak and beech compost quickly, while larger leaves, such as sycamore, take longer. Speed up the process by shredding leaves with a lawn mower, strimmer (make sure to wear eye protection), or special leaf blower. Borrow or rent expensive machinery from a gardening group to avoid buying it.

Creating the leaf mould

Drop leaves on to your pile and press them down firmly to make room for more. Mix in grass clippings to speed decompostion and add nutrients. Water the leaves if dry. Leaves compact when they break down, so don't worry as the pile shrinks.

FROM MID-OCTOBER ONWARDS THERE
SHOULD BE PLENTY OF FALLEN LEAVES TO
START MAKING YOUR LEAF MOULD PILE.
RAKE THEM UP WHEN THE GROUND IS DRY IF
YOU CAN, BECAUSE THIS MEANS THEY WILL
BE A LOT LIGHTER AND EASIER TO HANDLE.

GROW ON

SPINACH AND MUSTARD LEAVES

Prevent slugs and snails feasting on your autumn salads by going out at night and catching them in torchlight, or by baiting traps with beer close to your crops.

GROW ON

KALE AND SWISS CHARD

Protect your crops from pests, which will damage leaves as they grow. Pigeons, snails, aphids, and cabbage root fly all love kale and Swiss chard. Keep an eye on them, remove any troublesome pests, and cover your crops with netting if necessary.

GROW ON

KOHL RABI

This fast-growing crop does not perform well in dry soil, so water regularly during any dry spells of autumn weather to ensure the best possible harvest.

GROW ON

LEEKS

This tough crop (*see left*) needs little attention, apart from weeding around the plants. Removing weeds reduces the competition for the water and nutrients in the soil.

GROW ON

CARROTS

Weed carefully around carrots to avoid damaging the developing roots. This helps to reduce competition for the water and nutrients in the soil.

HARVEST

SPINACH

Now that your spinach plants have developed strong root systems and some mature leaves they will crop well for you. For the longest possible harvest period, pick only the biggest leaves from each plant once every couple of weeks, leaving the younger ones to grow on for later harvests. Continuous picking in this way encourages the plants to send up new leaves, and also means that if you only need a few leaves for a sandwich, then that's all you need to take. Picked young, spinach leaves are ideal for salads, while leaves left to grow larger are delicious when added to all kinds of dishes in the final stages of the cooking process.

HARVEST

MUSTARD LEAVES

Your mustard leaves will be ready to harvest this month. Simply pick the leaves from the outside of the plant as you need them, letting the developing leaves at its centre remain undisturbed to grow on for the next harvest. This will keep your row of plants productive for weeks to come.

   Asian mustards have a distinctive peppery flavour, which tends to become stronger as the leaves grow larger, so find the leaf size that suits your taste. Small leaves make a feisty and colourful addition to salads and sandwiches. If you find larger leaves too hot to eat when raw, try using them in stir-fries.

HARVEST TO TASTE
Pick smaller leaves for a milder flavour, or larger leaves for more heat.

HARVEST
KALE

At last your kale is ready to harvest! It can simply be picked as needed by snapping off the lower leaves a few at a time. Kale is remarkably hardy and will stand in the bed right through winter, so if you take just a few leaves from each of your eight plants at each picking, they will keep you going for months, even though they will now hardly be growing at all.

Kale is extremely nutritious and can be eaten raw or cooked in soups, stews, stir-fries, or pasta dishes. My favourite way to enjoy it is to tear off pieces of leaf from the stem before rinsing and drying them. I then rub them in a mix of olive oil, paprika, salt, and garlic powder, and bake them at 150°C (300°F) for 15–20 minutes, flipping them over halfway through. Delicious!

LITTLE AND OFTEN
I easily get carried away snapping kale leaves – they make such a satisfying sound!

HARVEST
SWISS CHARD

Remember that this second crop of Swiss chard will not have time to reach the mature size that your summer crop did. Pick the largest leaves on the outside of the plants when they are no more than 15cm (6in) tall. Snap or cut them off to keep a succession of baby leaves growing from the centre. If picked as smaller baby leaves, the bright stems of chard look spectacular in a salad. The larger leaves can be used in a variety of different ways, and are tasty steamed, stir-fried, or added to soups.

169

NOVEMBER

BEST THING ABOUT NOVEMBER
Plenty of relaxation and
hot chocolate to stay warm

WORST THING ABOUT NOVEMBER
Afternoons become almost unbearably short

WATCH OUT FOR IN NOVEMBER
Hard frosts that might damage
your spinach and Swiss chard

Leeks
These sturdy plants could be harvested now, but I save them for December

Kale
Your kale will provide plenty of nutritious leaves this month

Tatsoi
Harvest the outer leaves throughout November

Mustard leaves
Make the most of this peppery salad crop this month

Kohl rabi
Harvest once the stems approach the size of a tennis ball

Carrots
Pull up the bright roots and enjoy their intensely sweet flavour

Spinach
Continue to harvest early in the month, then stop picking and mulch the plants for winter

Swiss chard
Pick leaves early in the month, then mulch the plants to shield them from the winter weather

NOVEMBER AT A GLANCE

A quiet period begins in the garden now that the days are short and cool, and growth is almost at a standstill. Harvesting is the focus for most of the month, until the crops are finally spent. Once they are lifted, any bare soil should be "put to sleep" for winter under a thick layer of protective mulch.

HOW YOUR BED WILL LOOK
Early in November, the bed will be full of vibrant foliage. As the month progresses, the autumn crops fade and are gradually picked, leaving only the leeks and kale standing for winter.

ON THE PLAN
As the bed is prepared for winter, there are no newcomers. Rows of carrots, mustard, tatsoi, and kohl rabi will all be harvested and removed by the end of the month.

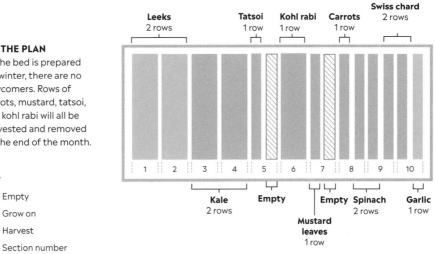

Leeks
2 rows

Tatsoi
1 row

Kohl rabi
1 row

Carrots
1 row

Swiss chard
2 rows

Kale
2 rows

Empty

Mustard leaves
1 row

Empty

Spinach
2 rows

Garlic
1 row

KEY
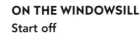
Empty
Grow on
Harvest
1   Section number

Garlic
Growth is happening underground this month. Shoots will appear in late winter

ON THE WINDOWSILL
Start off
• Sow microgreens successively in seed trays. Water and turn them regularly.

Harvest
• Cut your first crop of microgreens late in November, to add exciting colour and flavour to all kinds of dishes.

IN THE RAISED BED
Start off
• Activity has slowed in the bed as winter approaches and there is nothing to sow or transplant this month.

Grow on
• Apply a mulch to protect and enrich the soil around your leeks, being careful to leave a gap around the stems to allow ventilation and prevent fungal diseases.
• Wait patiently as your row of garlic starts into growth underground.

Harvest
• Pull up your carrots this month for a last burst of colour from the bed before winter.
• Enjoy the fresh, crunchy leaves of tatsoi in salads and stir-fries.
• Lift kohl rabi when their unusual ball-like stems reach 6cm (2½in) in diameter.
• Snap off the kale leaves from their main stem for soups, stews, and pasta dishes.
• Pick good-quality salad leaves from your mustard well into November.
• Continue picking leaves from your spinach and Swiss chard. Mulch around the plants when worsening weather causes them to fade.

MAINTENANCE CHECKLIST
• Remove any weeds before mulching.
• Mulch the bed.
• Compost all plant waste.
• Keep crops covered with netting to prevent birds from damaging them.
• Collect fallen leaves to make leaf mould.

173

ON YOUR

WINDOWSILL

There is nothing more to sow and transplant into the raised bed now, so this is the ideal time to grow microgreens. These tiny crops are fast and easy to grow indoors. Sow several types at once for a variety of flavours.

START OFF

MICROGREENS

SEED TO HARVEST
1–3 weeks

POSITION
Warm, sunny
windowsill

WATER
When compost
surface is dry

**HUW'S TOP
MICROGREENS**
Beetroot
Broad beans
Coriander
Peas
Radishes
Rocket
Spinach
Swiss chard

Microgreens are seedling vegetables that are cut when they develop their first pair of "true" leaves, which look like small versions of the leaves on the mature plant. They are nutritious, intensely flavoured, and, because they are harvested so young, can be ready in as little as a week. This quick cropping means that vegetables won't have time to form fat roots or pods, so you don't need to worry about which varieties you sow, although the variety will affect the colour of some leaf crops, like Swiss chard. Re-sow regularly for a supply throughout winter.

START MICROGREENS

Invest in a compost sieve to remove large particles from multi-purpose compost before sowing. This encourages seeds to germinate and grow evenly. Each crop requires a lot of seeds, but microgreens need little space to grow, so they can be sown close together. To keep costs down in future years, use leftover seeds from the previous year, or buy them in bulk (*see p21*).

1. Sieve multi-purpose compost into a large container. Throw the coarser particles left in the sieve o nto your raised bed. Use the fine sieved compost to cover the base of a seed tray to a depth of 5cm (2in).

2. Gently level the compost using your hand to create an even surface for sowing. Use your watering bottle with fine holes to thoroughly moisten the compost.

3. Sprinkle seeds thickly and evenly across the surface of the compost using your thumb and forefinger. Cover them lightly with 5mm (¼in) of sifted compost. Water the tray again, allow it to drain, and place it on a windowsill. Water when the surface of the compost looks dry. Once the seeds have germinated, turn the tray every day to prevent the seedlings from bending towards the light.

1

2

3

HARVEST
MICROGREENS

The seedlings are ready to harvest when they form their first "true" leaves, which look just like miniatures of the leaves on the mature plant. Cut the slender stems at the base with scissors, as you would cut cress. Microgreens are perfect added to salads or used as a garnish. The rest of the tray will continue to grow, but seedlings that have been cut will not produce new shoots – with the exception of peas (*see p41*). Once you have cut the whole tray, empty the contents on to your compost pile, brush down the tray, and re-sow.

FAST FOOD
Microgreens can be ready to cut as soon as one week after sowing.

175

IN YOUR RAISED BED

Harvesting your last salad leaves and root vegetables will be enough to keep you busy this month. Once they have been cleared, your final task for the year is to cover the bare soil with a thick winter mulch.

GROW ON

LEEKS

These have done most of their growing and are hardy, so are best kept in the ground through cold winter weather until you are ready to harvest them (*see right*).

GROW ON

GARLIC

Remember that your garlic is starting into growth underground, so take care not to disturb it while you are working on the bed.

GROW ON

KALE

Check that the stakes supporting the plants remain firm after any high winds, and watch out for pests. Keep the plants covered with netting to prevent birds eating the leaves.

A HANDSOME WINTER CROP
The long, blue-green leaves of mature leeks will make an attractive sight in the bed until you choose to lift them.

HARVEST

KOHL RABI

Now that they are ready to pick, you can see the strange form of these vegetables, with their ball-shaped stems sprouting long-stemmed leaves. They have a crisp texture and delicate, turnip-like flavour. Grate them raw into a salad with Swiss chard, spinach, and mustard leaves from the bed. Alternatively, toss them in a little oil and roast in the oven. You can also eat the leaves – prepare them as you would kale, by boiling, frying, steaming, or juicing.

HOW TO HARVEST

From the middle of November onwards, your kohl rabi will be ready to harvest when the round, swollen stems have reached at least 6cm (2½in) in diameter. Once they exceed 10cm (4in) in diameter they become less tender, so don't let them get too big. Pick by cutting the thin stem below the "ball".

READY TO EAT
Harvest your kohl rabi before they reach 10cm (4in) in diameter to ensure that they don't lose their flavour or become tough.

HARVEST
TATSOI

This unusual vegetable has a gentle cabbage flavour and lovely crisp texture. It tastes delicious raw in crunchy salads or lightly cooked in stir-fries, and it couldn't be easier to harvest.

HOW TO HARVEST

All of the plants in the bed will need to be harvested by the end of November, before the weather gets too cold. This means that you don't need them to keep cropping for a long period, so although you can pick the outer leaves from each plant as soon as they reach a usable size, as you've been doing with your other salad crops, you can also cut whole plants. To do this, cut the main stem at the base of the plant using a sharp knife, and discard any outer leaves that have been spoiled by slug damage before eating. Remove the row of plants at the end of the month by cutting all of the remaining leaves for the kitchen. Pull up the roots, shake off any soil, and put the roots on your compost heap.

HARVEST
CARROTS

Home-grown carrots, freshly pulled from the soil, are one of the best rewards for all of your efforts this year (*see left*). Their sweetness and strong, aromatic flavour will taste quite unlike roots that have been stored for sale in the shops, so make sure that you enjoy every single one.

HOW TO HARVEST

Your carrots will be ready to pick at any time in November, but the later you leave them, the bigger their roots will be. They should be easy to pull from the soil by holding the base of their leaves firmly and giving them a tug. If they are resistant to tugging, lift them with a hand fork, being careful not to damage the roots. Don't expect them to be huge, because they are a fast-maturing "early" variety that you've sown later in the year to squeeze as much productivity from the bed as possible. They will not need peeling – just a quick wash to remove the soil and they will be ready to eat raw, lightly boiled, or steamed.

CONTINUE TO HARVEST
KALE

Continue snapping off the lower leaves as required (*top left*). Don't forget that kale grows slowly in winter. I like to be quite reserved in my kale harvesting in autumn, to ensure there will still be plenty of fresh leaves for me to harvest and enjoy during the gloomiest days in January and February.

CONTINUE TO HARVEST
SPINACH AND SWISS CHARD

Keep picking the outer leaves from your spinach and Swiss chard plants until the middle of the month (*top right*).

At that stage, when there should only be a few leaves left, mulch the plants to protect them over winter (*see pp182–183*). In early March, remove and compost the mulch. As long as they didn't get extremely cold, your plants will begin to grow again.

CONTINUE TO HARVEST
MUSTARD LEAVES

The purple feathery leaves of mustard 'Red Frills' cope well with cold temperatures and should remain in good condition to harvest right through November. Continue to pick the largest leaves from the outside of the plants as required (*opposite*). Don't worry if flower stems grow upwards as the plants bolt, because these can be cut with a sharp knife and their strong peppery flavour is perfect for stir-fries. At the end of the month, pull out the roots, shake off any soil, and add the leaves to your compost pile.

MULCH YOUR RAISED BED

Mulching simply means covering the ground with a layer of either organic or non-organic material. Applying an organic mulch such as home-made compost during November is the perfect way to keep your soil healthy and your plants growing strongly, as it will increase the fertility of the soil and improve its structure (see pp204–205). It is like covering the soil with a cosy blanket, and is known as "putting the garden to bed".

In future years your home-made compost will be an ideal mulching material, because it will be rich in nutrients and organic matter. However, it is not yet ready to be used as it takes around a year to decompose properly, so in your first year you will need to buy compost or soil improver instead.

At the end of November, make sure your bed has been thoroughly weeded, then spread a thick mulch over the bare soil from section five on the plan to your row of spinach in section eight. Carefully apply a shallower layer around your leeks and kale, and a lighter mulch around the spinach and Swiss chard.

THE BENEFITS OF MULCHING

- Increases fertility
- Prevents rain washing away soil nutrients
- Stops weeds growing during winter, so the soil is ready for planting in spring
- Increases earthworm activity
- Removes the need for digging, because the soil organisms work the compost into the soil
- Increases moisture retention in the soil, making plants more resistant to drought

1

2

1. Empty a wheelbarrow or several buckets full of compost on to the empty part of the raised bed (section five to halfway across section eight). Spread it evenly over the soil using a rake.

2. Add more compost and continue to rake until this section of the bed is covered with a thick layer of compost, 8–10cm (3–4in) deep.

3. Lay sheets of cardboard over the compost to prevent weeds growing, and weigh the sheets down with large stones or bricks to prevent them blowing away.

4. Spread a shallower mulch of compost or leaves around your leeks and kale, to a depth of 4–5cm (1½–2in). Pull the mulch away from the plant stems to allow good airflow and prevent them from rotting.

5. Mulch your spinach and Swiss chard with shredded leaves or paper to a depth of 5–8cm (2–3in), lifting up the leaves and pushing the mulch underneath. Lightly water the mulch so that it doesn't blow away.

DECEMBER
JANUARY
FEBRUARY

BEST THING ABOUT WINTER
Hygge - the Danish tradition of enjoying
cosiness, good food, and good company

WORST THING ABOUT WINTER
There's hardly anything to do in the garden

WATCH OUT FOR IN WINTER
Heavy snow weighing down and damaging your plants

Leeks
The leeks will now have thick stems and are finally ready to be harvested

Kale
This plant just keeps on giving, as long as it isn't overharvested, so only pick what you need

Covered soil
Mulched and covered, the soil in this part of the bed will be absorbing its fresh supply of nutrients

Spinach
Protected by its mulch, this crop is waiting patiently to grow again in spring

Swiss chard
Like your spinach, your chard will die back now and flourish again in spring

DEC-FEB
AT A GLANCE

The only task to draw you outside on cold, dark winter days is picking your leeks and kale. The real work is indoors at this time of year, making plans for the growing season ahead. You can then order your seeds and sow heat-loving crops on a windowsill in February to give them a head start.

HOW THE BED WILL LOOK
All is quiet over winter, when the bed's appearance will hardly change. Your rows of leeks and kale will stand strong through even the harshest weather as the rest of the bed remains tucked up under its winter mulch. Watch out for the first garlic shoots pushing up in late winter.

ON THE PLAN

There will be nothing to sow or plant over winter, and the vegetables that are overwintering will stand quietly through the cold. Nothing will change on the plan until you start sowing again in spring.

Garlic
Some time in February you will notice the small, pointed green shoots of garlic emerging

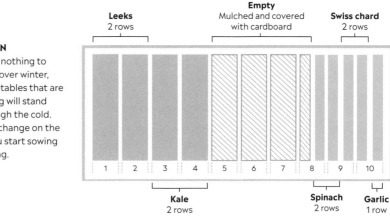

Leeks
2 rows

Empty
Mulched and covered with cardboard

Swiss chard
2 rows

Kale
2 rows

Spinach
2 rows

Garlic
1 row

KEY

 Empty

Grow on

Harvest

1 Section number

ON THE WINDOWSILL

Start off

• Sow heat-loving crops, such as tomatoes and peppers, on a warm windowsill in February to give them a head start.

Grow on

• Water and turn trays of microgreens to keep them growing through winter.

Harvest

• Cut microgreens as required. Empty the finished trays and sow a new batch of seed for another quick crop.

IN THE RAISED BED

Harvest

• Lift your first leeks after loosening the soil around their roots with a fork.
• Continue to snap off a few leaves from each kale plant as you need them.

MAINTENANCE CHECKLIST

• Weed.
• Water plants on the windowsill when the top of the compost is dry.
• Keep your rows of kale covered with netting if necessary, to prevent hungry birds from eating the leaves.
• Compost leaves, stems, and roots trimmed from your harvested vegetables.
• Knock any heavy snow from your kale and leeks.
• Wash your pots, seed trays, and tools so that they're ready for use in spring.
• Apply extra layers of cardboard on top of your mulch at the end of January if the first layer has started breaking up.

WINDOWSILL

Keep your windowsill busy throughout winter by sowing a succession of vibrant microgreens for quick harvests. You can also start off heat-loving crops in late winter, once you've made plans for the next growing season.

START OFF
HEAT-LOVING CROPS

SEED TO TRANSPLANT
18–22 weeks

POSITION
Warm, sunny windowsill

WATER
Every 2–3 days

TRANSPLANT
Late May or June

HARVEST
July to October

HUW'S TOP HEAT-LOVING CROPS
Aubergines
Chillies
Peppers
Tomatoes

Vegetables from hot, sunny climates, such as tomatoes (*see pp213–214*), peppers, and chillies, need a long, warm growing season to flourish and ripen well. This can make them difficult to grow outdoors in cooler regions. The key to success is to give them an extremely early start indoors during late winter to extend their growing season and give them time to mature.

Sow any heat-loving crops that you want to grow in the coming season on a warm windowsill in January or February. This will give you nicely established plants ready to harden off and move outside a couple of weeks after your last average frost date, usually in mid-spring to early summer, depending on where you live. This early sowing provides plants with two months longer to grow than those sown in spring, and will do wonders for your harvests. Just bear in mind that these plants will be large by the time they are transplanted, so you will need to pot them on into large pots as they grow, and give them plenty of windowsill space.

AN EARLY TOMATO SEEDLING
Heat-loving crops germinate quickly when sown on a warm windowsill in late winter.

GROW ON
MICROGREENS

Continue to grow a range of microgreens on your windowsill throughout winter for quick crops of intensely flavoured leaves (*see pp174–175*). I like to grow five types, such as peas, beetroot, radishes, spinach, and coriander, together in a "micro-garden", which gives me a variety of fresh food on the windowsill through the cold, dark months. Water the trays when the compost surface is dry, and turn them regularly to prevent the seedlings bending towards the light. As soon as a tray is harvested, brush it down and make a new sowing for continuous crops through winter. If your windowsills are get little or no sun, or you want to take things to the next level, invest in LED grow lights. These boost growth during winter and allow you to grow microgreens anywhere in your home.

PACKED WITH FLAVOUR
Fill your windowsill with densely sown trays of microgreens for a harvest of tasty shoots throughout winter.

IN YOUR RAISED BED

The only thing left to do in the raised bed through winter is to harvest your leeks and kale. You won't have anything else to sow, remove, or plant here until the spring, so enjoy putting your feet up for a while.

HARVEST
LEEKS

After waiting for what must seem like forever, you will finally have the pleasure of lifting your leeks. They are incredibly hardy, and will stand ready in the soil so that you can harvest them as you need them.
It may be tempting to try and pull leeks from the ground by their leaves, but this is likely to break or snap the delicious stem, which would be a disaster. The best way to harvest them is to push your fork into the soil about 10cm (4in) from the stem and gently pull it back to loosen the soil. You may need to do this on both sides of the plant to loosen the soil enough to pull the leek free. Trim off the long leaves and roots to add to your compost pile before taking your harvest indoors. Leeks have a stronger taste when freshly picked, and will make satisfying winter soups and stews.

A CHRISTMAS TREAT
Why not wait until Christmas day to harvest your first leeks, and enjoy something fresh from your garden for Christmas dinner?

CONTINUE TO HARVEST

KALE

Keep picking the outer leaves from each plant until only a small crown of about eight to ten leaves remains; let these develop before picking again. Continue to protect the plants from birds with netting. The stems will become longer as you pick your leaves, making the plants top-heavy. Add taller stakes if they look unsteady. When I remove kale in late spring, I crush the tough stems with a stone or hammer, so that they break down faster when added to the compost heap.

TASTY FLOWER HEADS
Kale plants will continue to produce leaves to harvest until late spring. You can then eat their delicious flower heads as a final crop.

ENDING THE GROWING YEAR

The end of one season in the garden naturally leads to the beginning of the next, and although spring can seem a long way off now, the dark depths of winter are the perfect time to be thinking ahead. The "Next steps" chapter that follows is filled with exciting new ideas to inspire your second year of growing your own delicious food. It introduces different crops to try, and collections of vegetables suitable for particular growing conditions. I recommend that you start thinking about your next growing season in December. That way, you begin the new year with a fresh plan and renewed enthusiasm for growing your own vegetables. This also gives you the chance to order seeds in advance, before stocks run out, so that you have them to hand when it's time to start sowing again.

NEXT
STEPS

So there we have it – a whole growing season has now finished. I really hope you enjoyed the experience of growing your own food. This next chapter is all about building on what you learned in the first year. It contains growing advice for several new vegetables, some alternative planting plans for you to follow, and some tips on how to maintain the long-term health of your raised bed. Hopefully it will help to give you the confidence to start creating growing plans of your own!

MORE VEG TO GROW

Your second year of growing vegetables is exciting as you can build on the skills that you learned in your first year, while expanding the range of vegetables that you grow. Even though we managed to grow a large variety of vegetables in the raised bed during the first year, I missed out a few of my favourites, so I have included them on these pages. There are instructions on how to start off, grow on, and harvest each vegetable, as well as varieties to try and some common problems to look out for (*see pp218–219*). Try working some of these vegetables into your plan for next year!

PLANTING PLANS

If you're looking for some inspiration for what you can do with your raised bed in future years, I have formulated four different planting plans, which can be found on pp196–203. Each has a different theme, such as a low-effort option, or a drought-resistant plan. The plans cover when to sow, plant, and harvest each vegetable as well as how much space they should occupy, working in the same fashion as the first year planner on pp32–33.

You may also want to start creating your own plans. Think about how much space your chosen crops will take up, how long they will be in the ground, and which crops follow on well from one another. If you find that you have some bare soil for a month, could you fill it with a quick sowing of radishes, or alter the timings of certain crops to maximize productivity? Use a colour system to clearly distinguish the difference between sowing, transplanting, growing on, and harvesting.

COURGETTES

These are tender plants that grow big, look impressive, and give high yields. They take up a lot of space: each plant needs an area of 90 x 90cm (3 x 3ft) in your raised bed. Alternatively, grow in a container with a diameter of at least 45cm (1½ft), rather than in your bed.

START OFF
Sow indoors at a depth of 2cm (¾in) in April to May.

GROW ON
Harden off and transplant when 15cm (6in) tall (May to June, after last frost), spacing the plants 90cm (3ft) apart. Water regularly; avoid splashing the leaves.

HARVEST
Pick courgettes when 25cm (10in) long (July to October). Pick regularly to extend the harvest.

KEY PROBLEMS
Powdery mildew

HUW'S TOP VARIETIES
'Black Beauty', 'Endurance'

PARSNIPS

These hardy plants are a delicious treat over winter, and taste best after they've seen a little frost. Plant two rows of eight stations per one-foot section of your bed. Rotate parsnips into your bed after potatoes, as harvesting potatoes loosens the soil, helping parsnips to develop large roots (*see p205*).

START OFF
Sow direct from March to May. Make 1cm (½in) deep holes spaced 15cm (6in) apart and drop three seeds into each.

GROW ON
Thin to one seedling in each cluster. Keep the soil moist and free of weeds.

HARVEST
Carefully lift the roots with a fork as needed from October. The foliage dies back over winter. Roots store best in the ground.

KEY PROBLEMS
Carrot fly

HUW'S TOP VARIETIES
'Gladiator', 'Hollow Crown', 'Tender and True'

FLORENCE FENNEL

Both the bulb and the leaves of this tender vegetable can be eaten. Plant a row of five stations per one-foot section of your bed. As your fennel could be harvested by July, be prepared to replace it with another crop, such as kale seedlings or turnips.

START OFF
Sow direct from April to July. Make holes 1cm (½in) deep, 30cm (1ft) apart; sow three seeds per hole.

GROW ON
Thin seedlings to one per station. Keep soil moist. Earth up bulbs when they start to swell (see p76).

HARVEST
Cut bulbs at ground level when they are 8cm (3in) across (July to October). Small shoots that appear later can also be eaten.

KEY PROBLEMS
Slugs and snails

HUW'S TOP VARIETIES
'Amigo', 'Finale', 'Sirio'

ONIONS

Home-grown onions taste amazing. You can start them from seed, but I grow mine from sets (immature bulbs), as it's faster and easier. Transplant a row of 11 onions into a one-foot section of your bed. Rotate onions into your raised bed after potatoes (see p205).

START OFF
Plant sets in individual modules in February. Half of each set should poke above the soil.

GROW ON
Transplant in early April, spacing the plants 10cm (4in) apart.

HARVEST
Lift bulbs when foliage turns yellow and wilts (July onwards). Dry lifted bulbs for two weeks in full sun before using them.

KEY PROBLEMS
Rust, Downy mildew

HUW'S TOP VARIETIES
'Centurion', 'Jet Set', 'Red Baron'

PURPLE SPROUTING BROCCOLI

A favourite of my sister, Fflur, purple sprouting broccoli is delicious. You should be able to fit a single row of three plants into a one-foot section of your bed. As your broccoli may not be ready for transplanting until June, sow a crop of radish or lettuce first.

START OFF
Sow seeds 2cm (¾in) deep in small pots from April to May.

GROW ON
Transplant one month after sowing when 10cm (4in) tall, spacing plants 40cm (16in) apart.

HARVEST
Cut central head before individual flowers open (October onwards, depending on variety). Harvest any side shoots that appear over the following weeks.

KEY PROBLEMS
Birds, Caterpillars

HUW'S TOP VARIETIES
'Cardinal', 'Rudolph'

SWEDE

This hardy vegetable grows well in a temperate climate, providing harvests during winter. Expect to get a row of six plants into a one-foot section of your bed. To make the most of the space in the bed, plant a quick crop of lettuce or radish in March, to be replaced by your swede crop in May.

START OFF
Sow seeds direct in a drill 2cm (¾in) deep from mid-May to mid-June.

GROW ON
Thin seedlings to 20cm (8in). Water regularly during dry weather.

HARVEST
Pull up the roots when about 10cm (4in) across from October to January.

KEY PROBLEMS
Powdery mildew
Clubroot
Cabbage root fly

HUW'S TOP VARIETIES
'Brora', 'Gowrie', 'Virtue'

PLAN ONE
COOL CLIMATE

Just because you live somewhere cool it doesn't mean that your vegetable growing has to suffer. In fact some crops, including brassicas, root vegetables, and salads, enjoy cooler weather. Plants are less likely to bolt (flower prematurely) in a cool climate, improving your chances of success and also letting you harvest salad crops for longer. If you live in a particularly cold area, start spring onions in modules indoors in February and plant your "first early" potatoes at the end of March.

Sow leek and kale seeds thickly in section ten in March, and then prick them out and transplant them into sections two to three and four to six in July.

Spring onions are a good vegetable to grow in a cool climate. Sow seeds thinly, 1cm (½in) deep, and then thin seedlings to every 2cm (¾in). Harvest the stems when they are just under 2.5cm (1in) in diameter.

ON YOUR WINDOWSILL

Month	Start off
March	Runner beans

IN YOUR RAISED BED

SECTION	MARCH	APRIL	MAY
1	**Lettuce** Sow	**Lettuce** Grow on	**Lettuce** Harvest
2	**Spring onions** Sow	**Spring onions** Grow on	**Spring onions** Harvest
3			
4	**Potatoes** Sow	**Potatoes** Grow on	**Potatoes** Earth up
5			
6			
7		**Turnips** Sow three 60cm (2ft) rows beside runner beans	**Turnips** Grow on
8			**Runner beans** Transplant into 90 x 60cm (3 x 2ft) area beside turnips
9			
10	**Kale** Sow thickly	**Kale** Grow on	
	Leeks Sow thickly	**Leeks** Grow on	

JUNE	JULY	AUGUST	SEPTEMBER	OCTOBER	NOVEMBER	DEC-FEB
	Carrots Sow	**Carrots** Grow on		**Carrots** Harvest		
	Kale Transplant	**Kale** Grow on		**Kale** Harvest		
Potatoes Harvest	**Leeks** Transplant	**Leeks** Grow on				**Leeks** Harvest
Turnips Harvest	**Beetroot** Sow	**Beetroot** Grow on		**Beetroot** Harvest		
Runner beans Grow on	**Runner beans** Harvest					
Kale Prick out **Leeks** Prick out	**Spinach** Sow	**Spinach** Grow on	**Spinach** Harvest		Mulch	

KEY ▨ Empty   ▢ Start off   ▢ Transplant   ▢ Grow on   ▢ Harvest

PLAN TWO
LOW
RAINFALL

Many regions go for long periods without rain during the growing season. Where water is available, plants can be watered regularly, but this takes time and effort. This plan contains crops that will be productive in hot, dry weather, without copious amounts of watering. Nearly all of these vegetables have survived three dry, summer months in my garden without any water and still produced decent harvests.

There are two vegetables in this plan that you may not have grown before: perpetual spinach, which can be grown in exactly the same way as Swiss chard, and parsnips, which are drought-tolerant, but will need moisture to germinate (*see p194*).

ON YOUR WINDOWSILL

Month	Start off
April	Dwarf French beans
May	Kale

IN YOUR RAISED BED

SECTION	MARCH	APRIL	MAY
1			
2	**Turnips** Sow	**Turnips** Grow on	**Turnips** Harvest
3	**Radish** Sow	**Radish** Harvest	
4	**Lettuce** Sow	**Lettuce** Grow on	**Lettuce** Harvest
5			
6		**Perpetual spinach** Sow	**Perpetual spinach** Grow on
7		**Parsnips** Sow	**Parsnips** Grow on
8			
9			**Dwarf French beans** Transplant
10			

JUNE	JULY	AUGUST	SEPTEMBER	OCTOBER	NOVEMBER	DEC–FEB
Beetroot Sow	**Beetroot** Grow on		**Beetroot** Harvest			
Carrots Sow	**Carrots** Grow on		**Carrots** Harvest			
Kale Transplant	**Kale** Grow on		**Kale** Harvest		**Kale** Mulch	
	Perpetual spinach Harvest					
						Parsnips Harvest in December
Dwarf French beans Grow on		**Dwarf French beans** Harvest				

KEY Empty Start off Transplant Grow on Harvest

PLAN THREE SALAD

A whole bed dedicated to salad will provide you with an amazing abundance of healthy greens throughout the year. I love growing salad, because it's so easy and the plants mature so fast. All of these leafy salad vegetables can be harvested using the cut-and-come-again method or by picking off a few leaves at a time. I designed this plan with early spring and late summer sowings, to be as simple as possible to manage, and also to give you a wide variety of salad ingredients to harvest.

Mizuna and pak choi may be new vegetables for you – grow them both in exactly the same way as you would tatsoi. Keep harvesting the leaves to encourage more to grow. Rocket is grown in the same way as you would grow mustard leaves.

ON YOUR WINDOWSILL

Month	Start off
May	Swiss chard
Dec–Feb	Microgreens

IN YOUR RAISED BED

SECTION	MARCH	APRIL	MAY
1	Lettuce Sow	Lettuce Grow on	Lettuce Harvest
2			
3	Spinach Sow	Spinach Grow on	Spinach Harvest
4			
5	Mustard Sow	Mustard Harvest	
6			
7	Pea shoots Sow	Pea shoots Re-sow and harvest	Pea shoots Re-sow and harvest
8			
9	Rocket Sow	Rocket Harvest	Swiss chard Sow
10	Radish Sow	Radish Harvest	

JUNE	JULY	AUGUST	SEPTEMBER	OCTOBER	NOVEMBER	DEC–FEB
		Lettuce Sow	**Lettuce** Grow on	**Lettuce** Harvest	**Lettuce** Mulch	**Lettuce** Grow on
		Rocket Sow	**Rocket** Grow on	**Rocket** Harvest		
		Spinach Sow	**Spinach** Grow on	**Spinach** Harvest	**Spinach** Mulch	**Spinach** Grow on
		Kale Sow	**Kale** Grow on	**Kale** Harvest	**Kale** Mulch	
Swiss chard Transplant	**Swiss chard** Harvest	**Mustard leaves** Sow	**Mustard leaves** Harvest			
		Mizuna Sow	**Mizuna** Grow on	**Mizuna** Harvest		
Pea shoots Re-sow and harvest	**Pea shoots** Re-sow and harvest	**Pak choi** Sow	**Pak choi** Grow on	**Pak choi** Harvest		
Swiss chard Grow on			**Swiss chard** Harvest		**Swiss chard** Mulch	**Swiss chard** Grow on

KEY ▨ Empty   ▢ Start off   ▢ Transplant   ▢ Grow on   ▢ Harvest

PLAN FOUR LOW EFFORT

Life can be hectic and leave you with little time to spend in the garden. If you are looking for a planting plan that's easy to follow, but delivers delicious vegetables throughout the year, then this is the one for you. There may be only five different crops, but each one is planted in quantity and can be harvested over a long period, so will provide you with plenty to eat. The key here is planting in succession in order to get two crops from the same space. Keeping the bed full of established vegetables will also leave hardly any space for weeds. I would always much rather grow food than weeds!

IN YOUR RAISED BED

SECTION	MARCH	APRIL	MAY
1	**Potatoes** Plant	**Potatoes** Grow on	**Potatoes** Earth up
2			
3			
4			
5			
6			
7	**Lettuce** Sow	**Lettuce** Grow on	**Lettuce** Harvest
8			
9	**Leeks** Sow thickly (in bed or on windowsill)	**Leeks** Grow on	**Leeks** Prick out seedlings
10	**Turnips** Sow	**Turnips** Grow on	**Turnips** Harvest

ON YOUR WINDOWSILL

Month	Start off
March	Kale

202

JUNE	JULY	AUGUST	SEPTEMBER	OCTOBER	NOVEMBER	DEC-FEB
Potatoes Harvest	**Potatoes** Harvest	**Kale** Grow on		**Kale** Harvest		
	Kale Transplant	**Spinach** Grow on	**Spinach** Harvest		**Spinach** Mulch for winter	**Spinach** Grow on
	Spinach Sow					
	Leeks Grow on					**Leeks** Harvest
Leeks Transplant						

KEY ▢ Start off ▢ Transplant ▢ Grow on ▢ Harvest

KEEPING THE **SOIL HEALTHY**

If you want to grow vegetables in your bed successfully year after year, you will need to keep your soil fertile and healthy. Adding a thick organic mulch annually is a must, and it is also a good idea to practise crop rotation.

NO NEED TO DIG

Vegetables need plenty of nutrients to grow and produce good harvests. The plants' roots take these nutrients from the soil, so it is vital to replenish them each year, ready for the next crop. Many gardeners do this by incorporating compost deep into the soil with a fork. There is another method, however, that requires minimum effort: it is called no-dig gardening, a technique that I learnt from Charles Dowding.

The appealing idea behind the no-dig method is that instead of digging in compost, you apply it in a thick layer over the surface of the entire bed each year (*see pp182–183*). Earthworms pull this organic matter deep into the soil, doing all of the work for you.

Digging also has disadvantages, because when you turn the soil, it loses its structure and brings weed seeds to the surface where they germinate. Mulching the bed prevents this happening and allows worms and other beneficial soil organisms to thrive undisturbed. This improves aeration and drainage, which promotes healthy root growth and nutrient availability to plants. Adding all this organic matter also increases the soil's moisture retention, making plants more resilient during drought. Building up a nutrient-rich layer of organic matter is a long-term project, but I have found the benefits to be incredible – just make sure to cover each part of your bed with 5–8cm (2–3in) of mulch or compost each year.

MULCHING BEATS DIGGING
There's no need to work hard turning your soil – simply adding a layer of compost to your raised bed will provide all of the benefits you need.

ROTATE YOUR CROPS

Crop rotation is a practice that farmers have used for centuries. It involves dividing up a growing area into defined sections, and then changing the type of crops grown in each section every year. Here are some good reasons for rotating your crops:

• It maintains a variety of nutrients across the bed, as each type of vegetable draws a slightly different combination of nutrients out of the soil.
• It allows crops to benefit from plants grown in the same spot the year before – for example, leaving nitrogen-rich bean roots in place for hungry brassicas.
• It reduces any build-up of disease in the soil where the same crop has been grown year after year, and keeps pests guessing where their favourite crops will be.

Don't worry too much about crop rotation in your second growing year, but do try to implement it from the third year onwards.

VEGETABLE TYPES

The key to successful rotation is to sort closely related crops into family groups. Members of each group tend to enjoy similar growing conditions and suffer the same pests and diseases, so should be grown and rotated together. Family groups are listed below:

• Legumes: broad beans, dwarf French beans, peas, runner beans
• Solanums: potatoes, tomatoes
• Alliums: garlic, leeks, onions, spring onions
• Roots: beetroot, carrots, Florence fennel, parsnips
• Brassicas: broccoli, cabbage, kale, kohl rabi, mizuna, pak choi, radishes, swede, tatsoi, turnips

Some crops don't require much rotation; these include cucurbits (courgette and squashes), perpetual spinach, salads, spinach, and Swiss chard.

FOUR-YEAR CROP ROTATION PLAN

This plan rotates over four years, and is the one that we use for the beds in our vegetable garden. Divide your space into four sections, and fill any available gaps with crops that don't require much rotation.

YEAR ONE

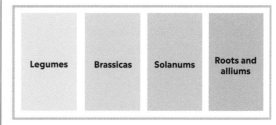

| Legumes | Brassicas | Solanums | Roots and alliums |

YEAR TWO

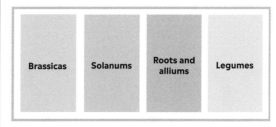

| Brassicas | Solanums | Roots and alliums | Legumes |

YEAR THREE

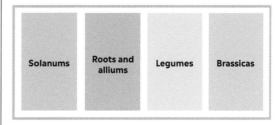

| Solanums | Roots and alliums | Legumes | Brassicas |

YEAR FOUR

| Roots and alliums | Legumes | Brassicas | Solanums |

VEG IN
CONTAINERS

This chapter covers how to grow a variety of different vegetables in containers. I love the flexibility of growing crops in pots, because you can easily move them around the garden, and they will add life and colour to an empty corner, patio, or balcony. Almost any vegetable can be grown in a pot, although you'll need to choose the right size and depth to suit each crop's needs. Containers need to be watered more often than raised beds, so many vegetables will need to be watered once a day during dry, sunny weather to ensure that you get a good harvest.

HERBS

Position pots of aromatic herbs close to your kitchen to create displays that are handy for picking. Combine annuals, which last a single season, with perennials, which last for years and are usually bought as young plants.

PERENNIAL HERBS

MINT

These hardy plants die back in winter, but will regrow each spring.

- **Transplant** In spring, pot on young plants into pots 25cm (10in) wide, filled with multi-purpose compost.
- **Grow on** Keep moist by watering frequently, and place in full sun.
- **Harvest** Pick the tips of stems, just above a pair of leaves.

ROSEMARY

Young rosemary plants (*opposite*) can grow into big shrubs.

- **Transplant** Move young plants into large pots in spring, using a gritty compost mix (*see box below*).
- **Grow on** Water when the top 5cm (2in) of compost are dry. Bring inside if temperatures drop below -2°C (28°F).
- **Harvest** Cut the stem tips about halfway down the soft, new growth.

THYME

Buy this compact, low-growing, hardy herb as young plants.

- **Transplant** Use a 20cm (8in) wide pot containing a gritty compost mix (*see box below*) to pot on young plants in spring.
- **Grow on** Only water once a week in summer, and less often at other times. It can be left outside over winter.
- **Harvest** Pick the tops of stems to promote bushy new growth.

ANNUAL HERBS

BASIL

A tender herb to grow indoors, or outside during a warm summer.

- **Sow** In spring, fill a 10cm (4in) wide pot with gritty compost. Sow eight seeds and cover lightly with compost. Water, and keep warm.
- **Grow on** Place on a warm, sunny windowsill. Water every two days.
- **Harvest** Pinch out the soft stem tips, just above a pair of leaves, when the plants are 10cm (4in) tall.

PARSLEY

Parsley enjoys moisture and is hardy enough to thrive outdoors.

- **Sow** Start in the same way as basil, but germination is slow. You may find it easier to buy seedlings in spring to grow on.
- **Transplant** Use a 20cm (8in) wide pot filled with multi-purpose compost.
- **Grow on** Water well when the top 1cm (½in) of the compost is dry.
- **Harvest** Pick the outer leaves, so that the central leaves keep growing.

MIX YOUR OWN COMPOST

Most herbs thrive in free-draining, gritty compost. To make your own, add one handful of coarse grit to every two or three handfuls of soil-based compost, and mix thoroughly.

POTATOES

Potatoes are one of the most productive vegetables that you can grow in a container, and are a treat to harvest. Growing these large plants in pots, rather than in your raised bed also frees up space in the bed for other crops.

PLANTING TO HARVEST
10–16 weeks

LIGHT
Full sun

HARDINESS
Frost tender

KEY PESTS
Slugs

HARVEST
June to July

HUW'S TOP VARIETIES
First early:
'Casablanca'

Second early:
'Charlotte'

Maincrop:
'Maris Piper'

The potato variety you choose will affect the time between planting and harvesting. Opt for "first earlies" for the fastest crops of baby new potatoes in about ten weeks, "second earlies" to harvest in around 13 weeks, or slower-maturing "maincrops" for large potatoes to pick after 16 weeks. Chit seed potatoes before planting, in the same way as you did for the raised bed (*see p49*).

START OFF
During March or April, plant seed potatoes into a large pot with drainage holes in its base. Ideally, choose a 30-litre (6½-gallon) container, but if you don't have one that big, find a pot with space for the roots to spread and form a good crop of potatoes. Durable growing bags also work well.

Add stones to the base of the container to improve drainage, and fill it halfway with multi-purpose compost. Space three seed potatoes evenly apart on the compost (*top left*). Cover them with 10cm (4in) of compost, water thoroughly, and place the pot in a sunny position.

GROW ON
Potatoes need plenty of water, especially when they are in full leaf and their tubers

are swelling (*top right*). Push your finger into the compost, and if the top 5cm (2in) are dry then it is time to water. Established plants will need the entire contents of a 10-litre (2-gallon) watering can every three days in warm weather. Rain will help, but don't rely on it, especially once the plants are fully grown, because then the foliage covers the compost and can direct droplets on to the ground.

Earthing up potatoes provides more space for tubers to develop, and prevents them from turning green and inedible when exposed to light. When your potatoes are in pots, simply wait until the shoots are about 5cm (2in) tall, and then add compost until the shoots are covered with a layer 5cm (2in) deep. When the shoots reappear, earth up the potatoes again, if there is space left in the pot for more compost.

HARVEST
To harvest, simply tip the pot out into a wheelbarrow (*opposite*) or on to a plastic sheet, and gather up the potatoes. Harvest new potatoes two weeks after flowering, or if you want bigger tubers, leave them for up to eight weeks longer. Watch out for potato blight in July and August (*see p94*).

TOMATOES

It is a challenge to grow tomatoes outdoors in cool climates, but their sweet flavour always makes it worthwhile. Place pots in the warmest, sunniest spot possible to maximize the chances of fruit ripening before summer ends.

SEED TO TRANSPLANT
12 weeks

TRANSPLANT
3-4 weeks after the last frost

TRANSPLANT TO HARVEST
Around 11 weeks

POSITION
Sheltered, in full sun

WATER
When top 5cm (2in) of compost is dry

HARDINESS
Frost tender

HARVEST
July to October

HUW'S TOP VARIETIES
Bush:
'Red Alert'
'Sweet 'n' Neat Red'

Cordon:
'Sweet Million'
'Sungold'

The easiest tomatoes to grow in pots are bush (determinate) varieties, which don't need to be staked; cordon (indeterminate) varieties will need support. Varieties with small fruits ripen fastest outdoors.

START OFF

In February or early March, sow eight seeds into a small pot, cover lightly with compost, water, and place on a warm windowsill. Put a clear plastic bag over the pot and seal with an elastic band, for extra warmth. As seedlings emerge, uncover the pot and keep it moist. Once the seedlings are 5cm (2in) tall, transplant them into individual pots (*top left*). Prick them out carefully, holding them by their leaves (*see p104*). To produce strong plants, bury the stem up to the first leaves. Water every day or two.

If you only need a few plants, buy seedlings in April. Keep them on a warm windowsill and move them into larger pots as they grow, until they can be planted out.

TRANSPLANT

Once there is no risk of frost, "harden off" the plants by acclimatizing them to outdoor conditions for ten days (*see p13*), before planting them outside. Choose 20–25-litre (4–5½-gallon) pots with drainage holes, or opt for growbags. Add a 5cm (2in) layer of stones to pots to aid drainage, and fill with multi-purpose compost. Squash growbags to loosen the compost before planting. Give your plants a sunny, south-facing position, ideally against a wall or fence.

GROW ON

Always water the pot slowly, until water flows from its base. Irregular watering can spoil the fruit, so check the compost regularly and don't let it dry out. Feed plants in growbags with an organic tomato feed once their first fruits form. Those in large pots can crop well without feeding.

Bush varieties need no extra care, but tall cordon varieties require support. Insert a 1.5m (5ft) bamboo cane next to the plant, push it down to the base of the pot, and loosely tie the stem to it (*top right*). Tie the plant in every 10cm (4in) as it grows. Snap off sideshoots that form between the stem and branches with your fingers (*bottom left*).

HARVEST

Pick tomatoes when they turn vivid red, or the specific variety's colour (*bottom right*). Eat them while still warm from the sun.

213

SALAD

Salads grow fantastically well outdoors in containers, and mature fast to give you quick crops. Make new sowings every few weeks and they will provide all the fresh leaves you can eat from spring to the end of autumn.

SOWING TO HARVEST
6–8 weeks

POSITION
Full sun or partial shade

WATER
When top 3cm (1¼in) of compost is dry

HARDINESS
Moderately hardy

KEY PESTS
Slugs and snails

HARVEST
April to November

HUW'S TOP SALADS
Kale (baby leaves)
Lettuce
Mustard leaves
Rocket
Spinach
Swiss chard

Salad plants don't root deeply, so grow them in wide, shallow containers to save compost and give you a worthwhile crop. Rectangular window boxes are ideal, but try wooden boxes, fruit and vegetable crates, lengths of guttering, or even old shopping baskets (*opposite*). Line gappy containers with hessian or a compost bag, and make drainage holes in the base of watertight containers.

START OFF
Sow salads directly into their containers from March until early September. Fill your container with compost to about 3cm (1¼in) below the top, and then thinly sow the seeds so that they are spaced roughly 1cm (½in) apart. Cover thinly with no more than 1cm (½in) of compost, and water the container well using a watering can with a fine rose, to avoid displacing compost and small seeds with large drops of water.

GROW ON
Salads will grow given at least four hours of sunlight every day, but produce the best harvests outdoors in the sunniest position possible. They may need to be moved into shade in hot summer weather,

however, to prevent their delicate leaves wilting in full sun. Keep the compost as moist as possible, and water when you feel that the top 1cm (½in) of compost is dry with your finger. Once the seedlings are 5cm (2in) tall, their roots will have grown deeper, and will only need water when the top 3cm (1¼in) of compost is dry.

HARVEST
After six to eight weeks your salad will be ready for picking. Simply cut two or three leaves from the outside of each plant, and the younger leaves at the centre will continue to grow for further harvests. You will be able to pick leaves for several weeks before growth begins to slow. When this happens, cut off all the leaves at the base of the stem for a final harvest, compost the roots, and re-sow.

TRY SOWING A MIXTURE OF DIFFERENT SALADS IN A LARGE CONTAINER TO GIVE YOU A VARIETY OF COLOURS, TEXTURES, AND FLAVOURS.

WEEDS

Your raised bed is a relatively small area in gardening terms, and this makes it easy to manage weeds. If you are ever unsure if a seedling is a weed or a vegetable, just allow it to grow for a little longer to develop "true" leaves (the second set of leaves that form after the initial pair). At this stage you will be able to see the difference between a neat row of vegetable seedlings and a plant wanting to capitalize on your healthy soil. A gallery of common weeds appears on these pages.

DEALING WITH WEEDS

Always stay observant and remove weeds as soon as you spot them. Use your hands if the weeds are small, or a hand fork to get under the roots if they are more established. Avoid raking or digging the soil for no reason, because this will bring weed seeds up to the surface and encourage them to germinate. Cover bare soil with a thick mulch and cardboard over the winter (*see pp182–183*), to help to prevent weeds becoming established. This will mean that your bed will be weed-free and ready for planting in spring.

STAY VIGILANT AND PULL OUT WEEDS WHILE THEY ARE YOUNG, SO THAT THEY DON'T DEVELOP A STRONG ROOT SYSTEM.

1. Hairy bittercress

2. Dandelion

3. Shepherd's purse

4. Annual meadow grass

5. Groundsel

6. Goose grass

7. Bindweed

8. Petty spurge (milkweed)

9. Dock

10. Stinging nettle

11. Ground elder

12. Ragwort

1

5

9

KEY **DISEASES AND PESTS**

DISEASES

1. Blight
This fungal disease affects potatoes and tomatoes, resulting in rotten harvests. Look for spreading brown spots on the leaves, and control by cutting off and destroying affected parts of the plant.

2. Blossom end rot
Erratic watering causes tomatoes and cucumbers to blacken and decay. Ensure you water plants regularly, and try to not to let the soil dry out between waterings.

3. Clubroot
This fungal infection affects brassicas. The roots become distorted and the plant is severely weakened, leading to poor growth and no crop. To prevent problems, rotate your crops annually and choose varieties that are resistant to clubroot.

4. Downy mildew
This fungal disease thrives in wet weather, when crops like lettuce can develop brown patches on their leaves, with mouldy growth on the undersides. Remove infected growth promptly and improve airflow around the plants. Try to avoid wetting the leaves when watering.

5. Powdery mildew
This fungal disease takes the form of white, powdery patches that appear on the leaves of plants. Powdery mildew thrives in dry conditions, so ensure that plants are kept well watered. Cut off and destroy affected parts of the plant.

6. Rust
Small, raised, orange spots develop (most commonly on the leaves), and the plant's vigour can be reduced. Remove infected leaves, and avoid adding too much nitrogen to your soil, as this encourages plants to make a lot of soft new growth.

PESTS

1. Aphids (blackfly and greenfly)
These sap-sucking insects distort new growth and eventually kill plants. Squash any that you find by hand. Encourage ladybirds into the garden to eat them.

2. Birds
Different birds often target certain veg: sparrows enjoy chard, for example. Birds can cause severe damage to crops, so protect your bed with netting, but check it daily for trapped birds (see p45).

3. Cabbage root fly
The larvae eat the roots of brassicas. Protect seedlings by covering them with horticultural fleece or using barrier collars.

4. Caterpillars
Caterpillars can completely strip the leaves of young plants. Use insect netting to prevent the butterflies from laying their eggs, and squash any caterpillars you find.

5. Flea beetle
The adults feed on the leaves of brassicas (see p205), peppering them with tiny holes. Young seedlings are particularly vulnerable, and should be protected with horticultural fleece until well established.

6. Leaf miners
These larvae burrow through leaves. Protect plants from egg-laying flies with insect netting. Rotate crops each year – if eggs are laid in the soil during autumn, flies may emerge under netting in spring.

7. Pea moth
The larvae get inside pea pods and eat the peas. Adults lay eggs on flowering plants in June and July, so cover crops with horticultural fleece during these months.

8. Slugs and snails
These slimy creatures wreak havoc on seedlings, especially on damp, humid nights. Tidy away any empty pots or other clutter that they can hide in or under, keep the grass short, and set traps (see p47).

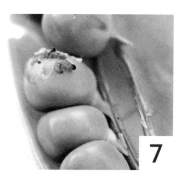

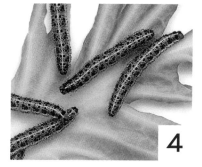

INDEX

SUPPLIERS AND RESOURCES

RAISED BEDS

British Recycled Plastic britishrecycledplastic.co.uk
Scaffolding Direct scaffolding-direct.co.uk

SEEDS

Organic Catalogue organiccatalogue.com
Real Seeds realseeds.co.uk
Tamar Organics tamarorganics.co.uk

TOOLS AND GARDENING EQUIPMENT

Bulldog Tools bulldogtools.co.uk
Gardening Naturally gardening-naturally.com
First Tunnels firsttunnels.co.uk

FURTHER READING

Allotment Month by Month, Alan Buckingham
Grow All You Can Eat in Three Square Feet, DK
How to Grow Winter Vegetables, Charles Dowding
No Dig Home and Garden, Charles Dowding
   and Stephanie Hafferty
The Vegetable Expert, Dr. D. G. Hessayon
The New Complete Book of Self Sufficiency,
   John Seymour

RECOMMENDED YOUTUBE CHANNELS

Back to Reality
Charles Dowding
The Gardening Channel with James Prigioni
Happen Films
Liz Zorab – Byther Farm
MIgardener
OYR Frugal & Sustainable Organic Gardening
UK Here We Grow

ACKNOWLEDGMENTS

AUTHOR ACKNOWLEDGMENTS

This book would not have been possible without the amazing support of my family and the team at DK. Firstly, a huge thank you to Publishing Director Mary-Clare Jerram, who made this whole book possible. Thank you to Toby Mann and Stephanie Farrow for their incredible patience with my haphazard content delivery, and for being so enthusiastic and helpful throughout the whole process. I also wish to thank the whole team at DK – Jo Whittingham, Maxine Pedliham, Christine Keilty, Glenda Fisher, Barbara Zuniga, Sophie State, Harriet Yeomans, and Geoff Borin – for making such a beautiful book out of the text and photos I gave them. And, of course, Nicky Powling, who designed the incredible cover! My deepest appreciation also goes to Bryony Fripp for the incredible raised bed illustrations, which really bring the whole book to life, and to Jason Ingram, who always made the photoshoots fun and relaxing (and who has also greatly inspired my own photography). I can't forget to thank my dad, Steven Richards, who taught and inspired me to grow food, and my mum, Clarissa, and sister, Fflur, who supported me through the whole process. Finally, thank you to my agent, Laura Macdougall, for being so supportive, and for being instrumental in getting this book published.

PUBLISHER ACKNOWLEDGMENTS

The publisher would like to thank Amy Slack and Dawn Titmus for their editorial assistance, Jo Hargreaves for proofreading, and Vanessa Bird for creating the index.

PICTURE CREDITS

The publisher would like to thank the following for their kind permission to reproduce their photographs:

(Key: a-above; b-below/bottom; c-centre; f-far; l-left; r-right; t-top)

11 Alamy Stock Photo: Peter Himmelhuber / Zoonar GmbH (bl). **Rex by Shutterstock:** Food And Drink (tr). **SuperStock:** Joseph De Sciose / age fotostock (tl). **34 Depositphotos Inc:** neillangan. **50 Alamy Stock Photo:** Hera Food. **62 Getty Images:** Adriana Duduleanu / EyeEm. **82 Sarah Cuttle. 98 Depositphotos Inc:** bhofack2. **118 Sarah Cuttle. 133 Alamy Stock Photo:** ergey Mostovoy (t). **154 Alamy Stock Photo:** John Glover (b). **156 123RF.com:** Evgenia Lysakov / karaidel. **161 Alamy Stock Photo:** Zoonar GmbH (crb). **170 Sarah Cuttle. 177 Alamy Stock Photo:** Photos Horticultural / Avalon / Photoshot (b). **181 Alamy Stock Photo:** Inga Spence (tr).

Images © Dorling Kindersley: 2; 6; 11 (br); 12; 14–15; 20 (cbr, fbr); 21 (bl, br); 22; 23; 24; 26; 42; 44; 45 (t, c, b); 59 (br); 60; 61; 74; 80; 81; 97; 107 (cr); 110–111; 116; 125; 134; 136; 141 (tl, tr, br, bl); 142 (tl, tr, br, bl); 143 (t, b); 145 (tl, tr, b); 149 (r); 151; 155; 161 (l, cr); 164–165; 168; 169; 175 (tl, cl, bl, r); 178–179; 181 (tl); 182 (tr, br); 183 (t); 184; 190; 194 (tr, br); 195 (tl, bl); 204; 209; 212 (bl, br); 215; 216 (tr, cr, br); 217 (tl, ct, tr, cl, c, cr, bl, cb, br); 218 (tl, tr, cl, cr, bl, br); 219 (tl, tr, tcl, tcr, bcl, bcr, bl, br); 224.

All illustrations © Dorling Kindersley

All other images © Huw RichardsFor further information see: www.dkimages.com

Penguin Random House

Editors Toby Mann, Jo Whittingham
Senior Art Editors Glenda Fisher, Barbara Zuniga
Designers Geoff Borin, Harriet Yeomans
Design Assistant Sophie State
Jacket Designer Nicola Powling
Jackets Co-ordinator Lucy Philpott
Pre-production Producer Heather Blagden
Senior Producer Stephanie McConnell
Creative Technical Support Sonia Charbonnier
Managing Editor Stephanie Farrow
Managing Art Editor Christine Keilty
Art Director Maxine Pedliham
Publishing Director Mary-Clare Jerram

Raised Bed Illustrations Bryony Fripp
Photography Jason Ingram, Huw Richards

First published in Great Britain in 2019 by
Dorling Kindersley Limited
80 Strand, London, WC2R 0RL

Copyright © 2019 Dorling Kindersley Limited
A Penguin Random House Company
Text copyright © 2019 Huw Richards
10 9 8 7 6 5 4 3
003–314040–Mar/2019

A CIP catalogue record for this book
is available from the British Library.
ISBN: 978-0-2413-7652-2

Printed and bound in Slovakia

A WORLD OF IDEAS:
SEE ALL THERE IS TO KNOW

www.dk.com

ABOUT THE AUTHOR

In 1999, Huw Richards moved from Yorkshire to mid-west Wales with his parents, who were after "the good life". They settled down in the foothills of the Cambrian Mountains, buying an 11-acre smallholding, which they transformed into an abundant, nature-rich environment.

At three years old, Huw was helping his parents in the vegetable garden. Aged twelve, he created his own YouTube channel, HuwsNursery, about vegetable gardening. He now has over 100,000 subscribers, and his videos have collectively been viewed over 20 million times.

Since finishing school in 2017, Huw has set out to help people reconnect with the food they eat and to empower them to grow their own food, be it on a windowsill, in a garden, or in a field. Huw also does a lot of work to inspire the next generation of growers, and hopes that every school in the UK can embrace gardening as a facilitator of learning and knowledge.

Huw has been featured in *The Times*, *The Guardian*, *The Daily Mail*, and on BBC News. He has also appeared live on BBC's *The One Show*. If he isn't in the garden or at his computer, he will most likely be playing tennis or squash.

Huw can also be found on Instagram at @huws_nursery.